SWEET HOME

SWEET HOME

OVER 100 HERITAGE RECIPES AND IDEAS FOR PRESERVING YOUR FAMILY HISTORY

REBECCA MILLER FFRENCH

PHOTOGRAPHY BY PHILIP FICKS

KYLE BOOKS

Published in 2012 by Kyle Books an
imprint of Kyle Cathie Limited
www.kylebooks.com

Distributed by National Book Network
4501 Forbes Blvd., Suite 200
Lanham, MD 20706
Phone: (800) 462-6420
Fax: (301) 429-5746
custserv@nbnbooks.com

978-1-906868-65-9

Project editor Anja Schmidt
Designer Lizzie Ballantyne
Photographer Philip Ficks
Food styling Roscoe Betsill
Prop styling Rebecca Miller Ffrench
Copy editor Liana Krissoff
Production by Gemma John and
Nic Jones

Library of Congress Control Number:
2011941332

Color reproduction by Imagescan
Printed and bound in China by C&C
Offset Printing Company Ltd

DEDICATION
**To my dearest treasures Anna and Camilla,
and to Jim, who shares my passion for
family and good food. It is you three who
make home sweet.**

CONTENTS

INTRODUCTION: DESSERTS MAKE A HOME

I come from a long line of dessert lovers. Recently reading some letters I had stored in the attic, I smiled as I found one from my grandmother with her typical signoff: "…must close. It's time to fix some coffee and have our evening dessert." It was a sacred bonding time my grandparents had with each other— and with sweets—every night around the time of the 10 o'clock news. Sometimes it was a few cookies, a piece of pie, or a luscious slice of chocolate cake, but always something sweet.

Sweets are in my blood; nearly every dinner during my childhood ended with dessert. I fondly remember my mother having some type of foil-covered treat— brownies, cake, bars—in the kitchen at all times. If there wasn't a pan on the counter, there was a pudding or custard in the fridge. Often the dessert was parceled out in individual footed glass bowls, ready to be served. (I'm still agog as to how my mother did this—she worked full time and had dinner and dessert on the table every night.)

Dessert is in my DNA; just like my grandmother and mother did, I've rarely let a week go by without a treat in the house (can't say I've always had dinner on the table, though!). Just as I remember my mother's warm, chocolatey pudding cake even more fondly than her meatloaf, I'm sure my own kids' memories of dessert will be equally vivid.

Dessert makes a house feel like a home, and my experience bears me out, as a child, as a parent, as a baker. Daily from the back seat comes, "What's for dessert, Mom?" And my kids aren't just asking on the ride home from school. In the morning, they're anticipating what lies ahead, knowing that after a long day, something comforting always awaits them on our cake stand. Am I worried about the saturated-fat intake of my family? Of course. But to be honest, the knowledge of a little tempting sweet at the end of a meal helps the spinach and squash go down without argument. Not that I'm a briber (although I suppose there have been times…), but in our house, within our family, and among many of our friends, baked goods represent a form of love.

SEASONAL MEMORIES

Baked goods also elicit seasonal memories. In the fall, the air is crisp and the autumnal light reflects off the leaves, glimmering gold and orange. I deeply inhale the lingering scent of smoke from a wood fire as I devour my mother's warm apple crisp—softened fruit under an oat and brown sugar crust with hints of ginger and cinnamon blending with a dollop of slightly sweetened whipped cream, melting from the heat of the dessert. The familiar flavors stir childhood reminiscences: Halloween, raking leaves, collecting bushels of apples, and family walks in the woods.

Fall becomes winter, the days are shorter, we spend more time at home, friends and relatives come and go during holidays. We cook and bake family recipes with many of those who visit: Mormor's rosettes, Robin's super-easy sugar cookies, my mother-in-law's legendary shortbread. When my husband, children, and I bake with other family and friends, we share secrets, learn new techniques, and create lasting connections.

For me, spring and summer also bring their share of nostalgic desserts: rhubarb crumb bars, strawberry shortcake, warm peach cobblers. Sweet memories are tied to vacations, celebrations, and special events, too: tiramisú, Jamaican sweet potato pudding, black-bottom ice cream pie. There's no birthday cake for my husband in August; instead, every year we serve him a strawberry-rhubarb pie with candles. While memories are individual, we all share the seasons and the bounty they provide—this creates common bonds among us.

DESSERTS—MORE THAN AN AFTER-DINNER TREAT

Sweets are made to nurture and comfort, and by no means should they be enjoyed only at dinner. I love serving fruity muffins or a fragrant coffee cake as the perfect finish to a mid-morning brunch. I know that when I pack unexpected cookies in my daughters' lunch boxes they feel an extra surge of love, or that placing a surprise sweet on a colleague's desk may lift his or her spirits. In my family, we're also big believers in the idea that celebratory events deserve celebratory measures. Birthday breakfasts may end with a doughnut tower alit with candles. I also love to overdo it at the holidays. Not just one, but two, three, or four desserts usually deck the table after a large festive dinner.

The tradition of weeknight desserts has been lost somewhere in the past 25 years. But times are changing, and so are family values. People are seeking inspiration from bygone times, when families weren't overscheduled or overprogrammed, when store-bought and readymade weren't common terms, and shopping wasn't a leisure activity. Families are looking to the past and seeking ideas for how to relish moments in the present.

The desire to reinstate the family dinner is part of this movement, and following a delicious meal, I believe, there should always be a sweet ending.

It's time to reconnect with each other—and those favorite, nostalgic desserts.

RECONNECTING WITH OUR PAST

I have always been interested in learning about my family's past. I knew I had some modicum of Norwegian ancestry, but until recently I was not sure in what regard. My mother's mother would make rosettes and *krumkaker* at Christmas, and my great-aunt Alice always made *lefse*. These Norwegian sweets seemed like our only tie to the old country—no one spoke or wrote the language or had any contact with relatives in the "homeland," as they so fondly call it.

I knew my father's side of the family was of German heritage, but the connection seemed somewhat tenuous. While all four of my great-grandparents on my father's side came straight from Germany,

they rarely looked back. There were few glimpses of Norwegian and German traditions throughout my childhood: My mother hung Scandinavian straw ornaments on the Christmas tree, my father hosted an annual Bokbier festival, my great-aunt knit wool socks for the Norwegian Seaman's Church, we ate wursts and schnitzels.

Then several years ago, my great aunt (my grandmother's sister on my mother's side) died. I was given her mother, Phoebe's, recipe journal. A worn, gray book with ledgerlike pages and the word *journal* printed on the front, inside were pages of recipes handwritten in my great-grandmother's script. Many were just lists of ingredients, with few how-to directives. The majority of the recipes were for baked goods.

I didn't think much of the journal upon receiving it, except how lovely it was to have such an old family book in my possession. Then a few weeks later I started really reading it, studying the entries, imagining my great-grandmother Phoebe cooking from these tattered pages that were once clean and new. Had she purchased this book or had someone given it to her? What was her kitchen like? Were kids running in and out as she cooked like they do at my house? Was her stove gas or wood? What type of pans did she use?

One fall morning I wanted to make apple cider doughnuts and was complaining that I couldn't find a good recipe. My daughter Anna, who greatly appreciates all things old and had pored over the old recipe book herself, said, "Why don't you try the doughnut recipe from your great-grandma's journal? Did you see it in there?" She was right. Why hadn't I tried any of the recipes from the book? And so I did, and it was delicious. There, under my nose, was a whole treasury of remarkable recipes.

This journal began an entire dialogue—the conversations that I'd wanted to start for years but hadn't. I engaged in long telephone talks with my grandmother, using the recipes as points of entry for discussion. The stories that unfolded were unbelievable; I learned of feuds, family traditions, and idiosyncrasies.

While I realized that my claim to Norway was somewhat distant at this point, it is, nevertheless, part of who I am—and this leads to my familial philosophy: Your history is your own and worth knowing. There are no rules stating that you have to be first generation to feel a kinship with a country from which you descended. Your history is the past, but also the present and the future. Just as the small remembrances of my family members are interesting to me, the legacy you create will be equally interesting to your future family and friends. Learning from the past may help you understand more about your family, why you harbor certain traits, or perhaps even why you come by things naturally. If anything, you'll most likely come across a few entertaining stories, as I did.

While there are many ways to research your personal history, one of the strongest ties a family shares is food: the traditional dishes, the ritualistic preparation, the celebratory table, and the personal conversations exchanged over meals. With the recipes in this book, I hope to inspire you to explore your own history through recipes and record it for posterity.

BREAKING IT DOWN

This book is divided into four sections: Preserving, Celebrating, Giving, and Creating.

Each chapter discusses ways to enrich family ties and friendship bonds with recipes and baking. While some families' histories may revolve around red sauce or rice and beans, my heritage was evident in the baked goods my family made.

I've learned there are many ways to preserve family ties. There need not always be the perfect photo album documenting each and every event. Instead, a favorite tangible item, say a kitchen tool or apron, artfully displayed, may provide more memories than a photo. "Preserving" will give you ideas for documenting your own family history.

"Celebrating" shares ideas for holidays, birthdays, and more. This chapter, packed with ideas for fun and easy dessert presentations, encourages you to re-create or carry on traditions so they may become a part of future generations' celebrations. There are several simple craft ideas for meaningful decorations that, when handed down, will carry with them fond memories and nostalgic reflections.

"Giving" includes tried and trusted recipes that are great for gift giving plus inventive ideas for wrapping, packaging, and sending sweets. I truly believe handmade presents embody the essence of giving, and continuing or creating the tradition of gifting homemade baked goods is a special way to share recipes.

In "Creating" I encourage you to start your own traditions. You need not come from a recipe-rich family or historically significant clan to make history. Your recipes reveal a lot about you. Share them, store them, record them.

Make the present count. Enjoy your family and friends always. Don't just wait for the holidays—make every day a celebration. Don't make desserts just for guests, bake often and let your senses succumb to the familiar smells and tastes. Use mealtimes and food to create daily rituals out of ordinary tasks, make them a time to converse and commune. Live, love, laugh—and appreciate being together. Make your home a sweet one!

BAKING NOTES

Although all desserts are comfort food by nature, the sweets in this book are especially homey. The cakes and pies will not resemble those in a French patisserie, finely glazed and cut with precision. Instead, these desserts are meant to be served on your great-grandmother's plate (possibly chipped, but that's okay), piled high with mounds of whipped cream, and perhaps even slightly askew. I hope some of these nostalgic recipes will speak to your memories and encourage you to seek out your own family's favorites.

I'm not a professional chef but a home baker. I've developed a portion of these recipes myself, but most have been acquired from family, friends, and others over the years. If you like something you're tasting, whether from a friend or relative or at a restaurant, don't hesitate to ask for the recipe. My favorite waffle recipe comes from the Lake Placid Lodge. I asked the waitress if the chef gives out recipes; she inquired and came back with the ingredients scribbled on a piece of hotel stationery that I still have today. Every time I use it, I think back to the sublime breakfast my husband and I shared in the Adirondacks.

Many of these recipes have been slightly adapted. Quite a few of my great-grandmother's baked goods called for lard or oleo, which I've replaced with butter. My mother's recipes would take certain shortcuts using processed products conventional for the time—pudding mix, Bisquick, canned German chocolate frosting—which I've replaced with homemade versions.

Most of my great-grandmother's recipes were nothing more than some combination of flour, sugar, baking soda, butter or lard, vanilla, and sometimes fruit or cocoa powder for flavoring. I've tried to improve on nostalgia by updating some of the recipes, like deepening the chocolate flavor with coffee, adding cacao nibs, or using fleur de sel. Yet I've also tried to preserve tastes that may seem unfashionable at present but very much worth a try, like date cakes, fruitcakes, and steamed puddings.

You may also find that some of your own retro recipes use unusual, or at least not very precise, measurements: one kitchen spoon (a teaspoon), a spoonful (a tablespoon), a pinch (what you can pinch between thumb and forefinger), a smidgen (even less than a pinch), a coffee cup (one cup), a scant cup (one or two spoonfuls less than a cup), slow oven (300°F), moderate oven (350°F). These approximations may seem frustrating, but take them in stride.

Although precision is key in baking, if you're prepared to test a recipe once or twice, you will usually figure out the correct proportions. It's important to archive changes and adaptations to preservation-worthy recipes. Be sure to have a pad and paper in the kitchen to record your trials every time. Do it while you bake or you're likely to forget what you've done.

Learning to bake from others is ideal. While books are excellent resources and great inspiration, standing beside someone in the kitchen and observing his or her technique is invaluable. This is a good time to take notes on measurements, carefully recording how much of an ingredient is used and when it's added. Observing friends or relatives bake is an excellent opportunity for spending quality time together. However, don't let the lack of a mentor hold you back. Use a book, experiment, or do what it takes…just start baking.

Bakers will inevitably obtain different results when following a recipe, even if just in presentation— perhaps the way the frosting is put on a cake, with peaks or spread smooth. When baking, don't hesitate to experiment with ingredients like nuts, chocolate chips, or coconut. If someone in your family dislikes pecans but loves walnuts, replace them, or leave them out altogether.

Notate any changes you make to recipes, which will serve as a reminder of preferences and personalities: "Oh, that's right: Da dislikes coconut." When you choose to tailor a dish to a friend or family member, you demonstrate thought and care.

I've kept these recipes fairly easy, and noted when one takes an especially long time or needs to chill or rise with the icon at left. There are recipes that require a food processor, and most call for a stand mixer.

Be creative when baking. If a recipe calls for a certain size biscuit cutter that you don't have, use a kitchen glass (like my grandmother does). If you're out of an ingredient, search the Internet for a possible substitution. One of my favorites is making whole milk (which we rarely have on hand) by using skim milk (which we always have) and heavy cream (place 1½ tablespoons cream in a 1 cup measure and fill the rest of the way with skim milk).

FLAKY PIE CRUST DOUGH

Easy as pie? Ha! Making pie used to make me nervous: What type of crust is best—all butter, some shortening, lard—how was I to know? My great-grandmother Phoebe had six sisters, and they would sit around for hours debating who made the best pie. Some pies have a thick top crust, bumpy from the filling underneath, others a thin, golden flaky crust, almost taut across the top of the pie dish. My personal favorite crust is a blend of butter and organic shortening: It's flaky, tasty, and holds its shape.

MAKES ENOUGH DOUGH FOR 1 DOUBLE-CRUST PIE

2½ cups all-purpose flour
1 teaspoon salt
1 tablespoon sugar
5 tablespoons cold organic nonhydrogenated shortening, such as Spectrum Naturals
10 tablespoons cold unsalted butter, cut into ¼-inch pieces
6 tablespoons ice water

1. In the bowl of a food processor, combine the flour, salt, and sugar. Pulse several times.

2. Sprinkle the shortening and butter over the flour mixture and pulse 8 to 10 times until the fat clumps are the size of peas.

3. With the processor running, pour the water into the feed tube. Stop the processor immediately and see if the dough sticks together when pressed between your thumb and forefinger. If it does, using your hands, shape the dough into two disks and wrap them in wax paper. If it doesn't, pulse a few more times or add another teaspoon or two of water. Do not allow the dough to come together in the food processor bowl. Place the wrapped disks in the refrigerator and chill for 1 hour before using.

A WELL-STOCKED
BAKER'S PANTRY

THE INTERNET IS THE BEST RESOURCE FOR MANY INGREDIENTS AND SPECIALTY ITEMS. HERE ARE SOME OF MY FAVORITES:

kalustyans.com | spices, flours

chocolatesource.com | cocoa powder, bitter- and semisweet chocolates

worldpantry.com | cacao nibs, bitter- and semisweet chocolates

Ghirardelli.com | 60% cacao bittersweet chocolate baking chips

macys.com | frango mints

kingarthurflour.com | maple sugar

indiatree.com | sparkling sugars

kingorchards.com | sour cherries

bazzininut.com | pistachios

ingebretsens.com | cloudberry preserves

Williams-sonoma.com | fleur de sel

bakeitpretty.com and fancyflours.com | baking decorations and paper goods

bakedeco.com and nycake.com | general baking supplies

sugarcraft.com | cookie cutters, lollipop molds and sticks

nordicware.com | spritz and krumkaker presses, rosette irons, bundt pans

hammertown.com | exquisite housewares

FOLLOWING IS A LIST OF ITEMS YOU'LL FIND USED IN THIS BOOK AND MAY WANT TO CONSIDER STOCKING:

baking powder and soda

all-purpose and cake flours

rolled oats

wheat germ

cornstarch

granulated sugar

light and dark brown sugars

confectioners' sugar

coarse grain sparkling white sugar

unsulphured molasses

honey

dry yeast

baking spray*

vegetable and canola oils

pure vanilla extract and vanilla beans

good unsweetened cocoa powder

bittersweet and unsweetened chocolates

instant espresso coffee

evaporated, condensed, and coconut milks

dried fruit (dates, cherries, coconut)

nuts (pistachios, walnuts, pecans), which I keep in the freezer

peanut butter

cardamom and nutmeg

ginger

cinnamon and allspice

* A word on baking spray: Butter burns much quicker than spray, so I use Baker's Joy for most everything unless otherwise noted.

A KITCHEN WISH LIST

While I find some kitchen equipment (a stand electric mixer) essential, others do not. Here I've made a wish list of sorts, including utensils and appliances that you'll see used in this book but that are by no means necessary for success. When a pie crust calls for using a food processor, you can use a pastry blender or two forks instead.

UTENSILS

liquid and solid cup measures
measuring spoons (I've been known to travel
    with mine)
wire whisk
wooden spoons
rubber spatula
offset spatula
rolling pin
small strainer

microplane grater
flour sifter
pastry blender
spring-release cookie dough scoop

SMALL APPLIANCES

kitchen scale
food processor
electric mixer
ice cream maker

PANS

12-cup standard muffin pan
24-cup mini muffin pan
11 x 17-inch baking sheets
8- and 9-inch round cake pans
9- and 10-inch round springform pan
8-inch square baking pan
9 x 13-inch baking pan
10- or 12-cup bundt pan
tube pan
5 x 9-inch loaf pan
9-inch pie plate or pan

Note on pans:

I find heavy aluminum pans the very best for baking.
I steer clear of nonstick ones, which are less durable;
the dark ones tend to make foods brown too quickly.
Cooking times should always be reduced when
baking with dark metal pans.

OTHER

mixing bowls
trifle bowl
wire cooling rack
candy thermometer
parchment paper
cupcake liners
pastry bag and number 18 star tip
kitchen timer
oven thermometer
rolling pin
rosette iron
krumkaker iron
spritz cookie press
assorted cookie cutters

PRESERVING

...a people without the knowledge of its past history,
origin and culture is like a tree without roots.

—MARCUS GARVEY

Preserving family history links one generation to the next. For my husband, my kids, and I, exploring our heritage gives us better insight into our family members. It helps us understand how they were affected by the state of the world during their childhoods, teaches us about cultures and traditions that have influenced our family, and, most important, gives us the ability to connect with family in the present.

My husband, Jim, for example, spent much time in Jamaica as a child. His father, Da (as his grandchildren lovingly call him), is fourth-generation Jamaican. Jim was 15 years old the last time he visited Jamaica. This past year, we traveled there with our two daughters, Camilla, 8, Anna, 11, and Da, who was 87 years old. What a trip! Seeing the country through the eyes of Jim's father was incomparable. We visited his childhood home, ate ackee and saltfish, and listened to his tales of being a young boy in this land. The girls sat wide-eyed as Da taught them to make nooses from banana leaves to catch lizards. We cooked sweet potato pudding with a local chef, and the girls will always remember making this dish with their grandfather in Jamaica—and will surely share this recipe and memory with their kids one day.

Trips like this don't happen often, but you need not travel to some far-off destination to re-create recipes or revive memories. Your own kitchen is the perfect setting. Arousing your senses will surely prompt reminiscences.

Scent is a powerful—and instinctual—sense. Animals can navigate home by scent, and a familiar aroma of a favorite dessert may transport you to a memorable place. Taste has the ability to create strong associations too. Even the sight of a beloved dish may stir memories—we begin to imagine the taste of something with our eyes long before it enters our mouth.

Your first step in preserving family history through recipes is to ask yourself why you want to do it. Have you been saving family recipes for years? Is there a lost family recipe that you'd like to resurrect? Do you want to bring family stories to light? Or is your interest strictly technique-driven—what to do with that antique rosette iron that was your grandmother's?

Perhaps you don't even know the reason—as they say, the journey is as valuable as reaching the destination. Whatever your goal, here are a few ways to get started preserving your family's history.

READY, SET...PREP

GET YOUR HANDS DIRTY AND START DIGGING

Literally, head for basements and attics—your own, your parents', your aunts' and uncles'. Look for old recipe boxes, notebooks, cookbooks, and letters. I found a notebook of my mother-in-law's stashed with her old cookbooks. The notebook contained Christmas lists dating back many years, as well as some recipes she'd given as gifts. It reminded me of one of my favorite gifts from her: a balsamic reduction that she'd made and jarred herself (long before balsamic glaze was available in grocery stores), to which she attached the recipe typed on an index card. I had long since misplaced the card and was thrilled to come across the recipe again. Collect everything you can find and ask to borrow it.

KEEP YOUR EYES OUT FOR BAKING ACCOUTREMENTS

Look in the backs of cupboards or closets for forgotten shortbread molds, pudding molds, cookie cutters, cake stands, cookie jars, pizzelle irons, *krumkaker* presses, rosette irons, bundt pans, wire whisks, and even wooden and silver spoons. Old aprons and tea towels may stir up some memories too. Recently one night after dinner, my husband was washing a small, white spouted saucepan. He looked up and said, "Was this my mother's?" Indeed it was, and its distinctive appearance took Jim immediately back to his own childhood kitchen.

A PICTURE'S WORTH A THOUSAND WORDS

While I have more photos than I know what to do with, past generations did not. Ask family members if you can borrow any food-related pictures, which could include photos of relatives cooking, their kitchens, gardens, holiday meals, or other family gatherings.

BY ALL MEANS, DON'T HOARD OR STOCKPILE

Bequeathal can become a touchy subject fast. "But Grandma promised me her bunny cake mold." "I get the rolling pin. I've used it more than any of *you*!" And so the stories go. I've even seen family members who *don't* bake or cook get territorial over kitchen equipment and cookbooks. So here's my advice: Be generous. If there are disagreements over who should have the pizzelle iron, suggest one person house it and host an annual pizzelle-making get-together so everyone will get a chance to use it. Be the bigger person and find another one online or in a second-hand store. If you are the one lucky enough to possess it, share it, use it, and proudly display it.

When borrowing recipes, notebooks, or photos, make copies and offer to make them for other family members as well. Treat these items with respect and return then in a timely manner so you're given future access to family documents.

SORT AND SIFT

ENLIST A FAMILY MEMBER When sifting through recipes and photos, ask a relative to join you, one who is familiar with your family's history. Take notes while you're working. Consider sorting your finds by generation, or by decade. When I started exploring my great-grandmother's journal, many questions came to mind. It's important to write them down as you have them. Record your discoveries in a fact-finding journal or notebook.

ASK, ASK, AND ASK SOME MORE Should I say it again? Never hesitate to ask. Most people love talking about themselves. A friend of mine who always knows the inside scoop on everything is actually a very reserved person. She says she just sits back and listens. And that's the key to learning: listening. Take the time to hear what you're being told. It seems funny to say, but in this time of sound bytes and taglines, people don't always truly engage, they answer phones, check emails, and look at screens instead of concentrating 100 percent on each other. Set up informal interviews with relatives by phone, in person, or by written correspondence to find out more about your family's history.

HERE ARE A FEW GENERAL INTERVIEW QUESTIONS TO GET YOU STARTED:

1. What was your childhood kitchen like? Did you spend much time there?
2. What's your all-time favorite baked good? Why?
3. Did you have family meals growing up? If so, what were they like?
4. If you bake or cook, do you remember your first experience in the kitchen?
5. What food did you eat at home that was traditional to your heritage? Do you still make and/or eat it/them today? If not, why not? If so, what memories does that dish or item evoke?
6. What was your favorite celebratory family gathering? Why?

MAP IT OUT Once I started asking questions, unfamiliar names were being mentioned again and again. "Wait, whose sister was she again?" "Was that your uncle on your mother's or father's side?" I felt like I was trying to memorize verb conjugations in a foreign language. I finally asked a relative to map out our family tree for reference. If you don't already have access to one, there are many online programs and genealogical sites to help you create your own family tree.

PRESERVE

Once you've done some sleuthing, it's likely you will have found some information or items with which to do some artful archiving. Here are 10 suggestions for preserving your family recipes and more.

1. COPY, PROTECT, STORE It's most important to ensure that original recipes are kept in a dry, safe place. Store them in an archival box (lightingimpressions.com is one of my favorite sources) and keep copies on hand for cooking. Laminate copies of your favorite recipes on cards and fasten them in the corner to create a fanlike collection for a great gift. Or scan original recipes and burn them onto CDs to share.

2. PRODUCE A VIDEO DVD Videotaping a cook in the act is one of the best ways to preserve a relative's baking method—don't hesitate to ask him or her to use your set of measuring cups instead of approximating amounts. Shoot the recipes and food-related photos as well. There are online sites that will put together a production for you; check out familymemoriesvideo.com and littledreampictures.com.

3. RECORD A LIVE INTERVIEW Some people are less intimidated by voice recording: Book a live interview with a relative, asking him or her to describe a family dish, and use a digital recorder to make a sound recording. Use the questions opposite and compose some of your own in advance.

4. DESIGN AN ACCORDION-FOLD HOW-TO ALBUM Work with a family member to document your favorite recipe. Take a photo of each step, writing down helpful notes along the way. Display those photos and notes in an accordion book (available from ragandbonebindery.com) for a fun, how-to presentation.

5. MAKE A SET OF NOTECARDS Create customized notecards featuring a recipe. Cafepress.com offers several options in its design-your-own section. Take a photo of the baked good to use for the card's front and print the recipe inside. If you have old handwritten recipes, consider using scans of them, too.

6. CREATE A SHADOWBOX Display keepsake items that won't fit in scrapbooks on your kitchen wall using a deep, glass-fronted frame. Pair items you'd like to preserve, such as an heirloom silver spoon or an apron, with a favorite recipe card and photo. Line the back of the box frame with colorful paper.

7. MAKE A MAGNETIC RECIPE BOARD Using a cookie sheet and a display-worthy recipe, create a memo board on which you can hang other recipes. Hand-lettering and illustrations available from nancyhowell.com.

8. PAPERLESS RECIPE PRESERVATION Do you remember those vintage tea towels with recipes printed on them? You can easily create a set using your own recipes. Print a recipe on a tea towel or apron at zazzle.com, or illustrate a recipe and transfer it to a pie plate or platter at customsepia.com.

9. START A FAMILY RECIPE BLOG This forum instantly connects family members who are separated by great distances and gives everyone a chance to tell his or her story. The minute you start posting, your history is electronically preserved. Wordpress.com or blogger.com are good places to get started.

10. WRITE A COOKBOOK There are many online companies that specialize in cookbook production; I like lulu.com and blurb.com. Include photos, quotes, personal stories, and changes that have been made to recipes over time. Scanned children's illustrations, old letters, and newspaper clippings are great too.

GREAT-GRANDMA'S CHOCOLATE DATE CAKE

On the torn, stained pages of my great-grandmother's journal are many recipes using dates: There are four types of bars, cookies, fillings, and a cake. I asked my mother why she doesn't bake with dates, she told me she used to, but guessed my sister and I didn't like them and stopped using them. "In fact," she said, "our groom's cake was a date cake. Grandma insisted we have one at our wedding."

Not knowing what to expect, I made the cake, as directed by my mother. This modest cake may not have a glossy buttercream or show-stopping fruit topping, but it does have a memorably rich, ambrosial flavor. The super-moist crumb has a gratifying chocolate taste. I doubt most tasters of this cake will recognize the dates, and will instead ask what makes the cake so moist. Dates are higher in potassium than bananas and higher in antioxidants than blueberries, and packed with health benefits. If you are on the fence about dates, I encourage you to try this cake—it's extremely tasty and will restore dates to their rightful place in your baker's pantry.

SERVES 12 TO 14

1 cup chopped dates
1 cup boiling water
1 teaspoon baking soda
8 tablespoons (1 stick) unsalted butter
1 cup firmly packed light brown sugar
1 large egg
1 1/2 cups all-purpose flour
1 tablespoon unsweetened cocoa powder
1/2 teaspoon salt
1 teaspoon pure vanilla extract
1 1/4 cups semisweet chocolate chips
1/2 cup chopped walnuts (optional)

1. Preheat the oven to 350°F. Grease and flour a 10-inch springform pan using baking spray.

2. Put the dates in a small bowl and pour the boiling water over them. Let stand completely covered in water until cool, then stir in the baking soda.

3. In the bowl of a stand mixer fitted with the paddle attachment, cream the butter and brown sugar until light and fluffy, about 3 minutes.

4. Add the egg and mix until combined, scraping down the sides of the bowl as necessary.

5. Slowly add the flour, cocoa powder, and salt and beat on low. Increase the speed to medium and beat until thoroughly incorporated, about 30 seconds. Add the vanilla extract and beat to combine. Stir in the date mixture, including all the unabsorbed water. Stir in 3/4 cup of the chocolate chips.

6. Pour the mixture into the prepared pan. Combine the remaining 1/2 cup chocolate chips and the walnuts, if desired, in a small bowl and spoon over the cake.

7. Bake for 35 minutes, or until a toothpick inserted in the center comes out clean and the top of the cake springs back when gently pressed with your finger. Allow the cake to cool completely in the pan. Gently open the springform pan and serve.

GERMAN APPLE CUSTARD CAKE

At some point every spring during my childhood, my parents would announce: "Time for the Bockbierfest!" Their own version of a Bavarian bierfest, this lively gathering of friends and family was a celebration of my father's German heritage. Bockbier, which is brewed in the winter for spring consumption, was the center of the somewhat raucous affair, complete with oom-pah tunes, lederhosen, and dirndls. As with most celebrations, in the end, it's all about the food: liverwurst, herring, bratwurst and knockwurst, sauerkraut, *kartoffelsalat* (German potato salad), and my favorite, German Apple Custard Cake. This dessert, with a cakelike crust, is layered with sliced apples, topped with a cream mixture that sets to a smooth custard when baked, and finished with small mounds of dough that create a golden, cobbled top crust. The cake bakes for almost an hour, and needs to set for another hour or so, but like bockbier it gets better as it stands.

SERVES 10 TO 12

3 Granny Smith apples (about 1 pound), peeled, cored, and thinly sliced

1 tablespoon lemon juice

1 teaspoon grated lemon zest

12 tablespoons (1 1/2 sticks) unsalted butter, at room temperature

3/4 cup plus 3 tablespoons sugar

1 1/2 cups plus 1 tablespoon all-purpose flour

1/2 teaspoon salt

3 large eggs, at room temperature

1 cup heavy cream

1 teaspoon pure vanilla extract

1 teaspoon pure almond extract

1 vanilla bean

2 tablespoons blanched sliced almonds

1. Preheat the oven to 350°F. Grease a 9-inch round springform pan with baking spray.

2. In a bowl, stir together the apple slices, lemon juice, and zest. Set aside.

3. In the bowl of a stand mixer fitted with the paddle attachment, cream the butter and 1/4 cup plus 2 tablespoons sugar until light and fluffy, about 3 minutes. With the mixer on low, slowly add 1 1/2 cups of the flour and the salt. Beat for 30 seconds, scraping down the sides of the bowl as necessary, until a dough is formed.

4. Remove about 1 1/3 cups of dough from the bowl and firmly press it into the prepared pan. The crust will seem thin and will just cover the bottom of the pan. Arrange the prepared apple slices in an overlapping, circular pattern on top of the dough in the pan.

5. Add 1 egg to the remaining dough in the bowl. Mix on low until fully incorporated, about 20 seconds, scraping down the sides of the bowl as necessary.

6. In a medium bowl, lightly whisk together the remaining 2 eggs, the cream, 1 tablespoon flour, and the vanilla and almond extracts. Split the vanilla bean lengthwise and scrape the seeds into the cream mixture. Add 1/2 cup sugar and continue whisking until smooth. Pour the mixture over the apples.

7. Using a few teaspoon- and tablespoon-size scoops, drop the egg-flour mixture evenly over the apples in a cobbled pattern. Sprinkle the almonds and remaining 1 tablespoon sugar over the entire top of the cake. Bake for 55 to 60 minutes, until the cobbled top is pale golden and a very slight brown color edges the pan. Let the cake cool in the pan for at least 1 hour before serving.

MARYANN'S FUDGE PECAN PIE

My mother, MaryAnn, hates a mess. You'll never find her frying doughnuts or rosettes like my grandmother does. The spattering grease makes her twitch. She's very orderly in the kitchen, which is one reason she loves pies. One floury, disorderly moment while she rolls out the pie dough, she cleans up, and she's done. My mother's adoration for pies is not only in the process, but the finished product. She likes the flaky crust balanced by a luscious filling. This Fudge Pecan Pie, laden with nuts and chocolate, is the perfect example. The sweetness of traditional pecan pie is dialed down here by the addition of cocoa powder and the use of Lyle's Golden Syrup, which is more flavorful than corn syrup. Those two ingredients create a thick, fudgy filling that is ultra-decadent. Because the pie is so rich, serve very thin slivers accompanied by a scoop of coffee, caramel, or vanilla ice cream (or a little tablespoon of each). Whipped cream is good too.

SERVES 16

1 batch Flaky Pie Crust Dough (page 11)

1/2 cup firmly packed light brown sugar

One 11-ounce bottle Lyle's Golden Syrup (about 1 1/3 cups)*

1/3 cup unsweetened cocoa powder

1/3 cup all-purpose flour

3 large eggs

3 tablespoons unsalted butter, melted

1/2 teaspoon salt

2 teaspoons pure vanilla extract

3/4 cup chopped pecans, plus 1 cup pecan halves

* Lyle's Golden Syrup, imported from the UK and made from pure sugar cane, can be found at specialty stores or online. You can use light corn syrup as a substitute here.

1. Preheat the oven to 350°F.

2. Roll out the Flaky Pie Crust dough on a lightly floured surface to a 12-inch circle. Transfer to a 9-inch pie pan and flute or crimp the edges. Refrigerate until ready for use.

3. In the bowl of a stand mixer fitted with the whisk attachment, combine the brown sugar, golden syrup, cocoa powder, and flour on medium until thoroughly mixed, about 30 seconds. Add the eggs, melted butter, salt, and vanilla extract and mix on medium for 1 minute, or until all the ingredients are fully incorporated. Stir in the chopped pecans with a wooden spoon.

4. Remove the pie crust from the refrigerator and pour the mixture into the prepared pan. Arrange the pecan halves in a circular fashion on the surface of the pie.

5. Bake for 1 hour, or until a knife inserted into the center of the pie comes out clean.

6. Let the pie cool completely before serving. To allow the full flavor to develop, cook the pie one day in advance and cover at room temperature until ready to serve.

MOLASSES COOKIE
ICE CREAM SANDWICHES

Gingersnaps, molasses crinkles, gingerbread cookies. Like the thousand-plus varieties of apples in this world, there must be as many variations of the molasses cookie—some chewy, some crisp, some thick, some thin. In her humble journal, great-grandma Phoebe had no fewer than four recipes for ginger cookies. This one is particularly small, soft, and somewhat spicy due to the addition of white pepper. While many may associate this fragrant sweet with the holidays, there's no reason to deny yourself the rest of the year. This versatile bite-size cookie is as pleasant in summer as in winter—especially when two sandwich a tiny scoop of vanilla ice cream.

**MAKES 2 1/2 TO 3 DOZEN
ICE CREAM SANDWICHES**

4 cups all-purpose flour

1 tablespoon ground ginger

1/2 teaspoon cinnamon

1/8 teaspoon ground white pepper

1/2 teaspoon salt

1 teaspoon baking soda

8 ounces (2 sticks) unsalted butter,
   at room temperature

1 cup sugar

1 cup unsulphured molasses (not robust)

1 teaspoon pure vanilla extract

1 pint vanilla ice cream

1. In a bowl, stir together the flour, ginger, cinnamon, white pepper, salt, and baking soda until thoroughly mixed.

2. In the bowl of a stand mixer fitted with the paddle attachment, cream the butter and 1/2 cup of the sugar on medium-high for 4 minutes, or until light and fluffy, scraping down the sides of the bowl as necessary. Add the molasses and vanilla extract and beat until combined, continuing to scrape the sides of the bowl.

3. Turn the mixer off and add the dry ingredients. With the mixer on low, mix until just combined. Cover the dough with plastic wrap and chill for at least 2 hours or overnight.

4. Preheat the oven to 350°F. Line two baking sheets with parchment paper.

5. Remove the dough from the refrigerator. Using a teaspoon measure, scoop out a small ball of dough, roll it between the palms of your hands, and then roll it in the remaining 1/2 cup sugar. Repeat with the rest of the dough. (The balls will seem very small, but keep in mind they make bite-size cookie sandwiches.) Place the balls 2 inches apart on the prepared baking sheet. Slightly flatten (not too much; just so they're about 1/4 inch thick) with the flat bottom of a measuring cup or spatula.

6. Bake for 10 to 12 minutes. The cookies are meant to be soft; they will not brown, just be slightly cracked. Let cool for 5 minutes on the baking sheet then, using a spatula, transfer to a wire cooling rack.

7. When the cookies have cooled, pair them according to size. Place a small scoop of ice cream on the flat side of one cookie and sandwich with another. Serve immediately.

PEANUT BUTTER POPPER COOKIES

This recipe from my great-grandmother's journal had no directions nor oven temperatures, just a list of ingredients. My grandmother filled in the blanks and instructed me to replace the lard, which the list included, with butter. She said during the Depression they baked with lard because it was cheaper, and added, "It was really only good when we got it from local farmers, who rendered their own." Relieved I don't have to seek out hand-rendered lard, I did make an addition that seems somewhat decadent, given that it's hand-harvested from salt ponds in France and wasn't readily available during my great-grandmother's less prosperous times: fleur de sel. A pinch of this delicate salt atop these bite-size cookies makes them burst with flavor. Now a part of my repertoire, these addictive cookies are lovingly called poppers for my husband, who, when the cookie jar is full of these, can't stop popping the small, soft peanut butter bites into his mouth.

MAKES ABOUT 5 DOZEN COOKIES

3 cups all-purpose flour

1 teaspoon baking soda

1/4 teaspoon salt

12 tablespoons (1 1/2 sticks) unsalted
   butter, at room temperature

1 cup chunky peanut butter

1 cup sugar

1 cup firmly packed light brown sugar

2 large eggs, at room temperature

1/4 cup milk

1 teaspoon pure vanilla extract

1 tablespoon fleur de sel*

* You may substitute another type
   of crystalline sea salt.

1. Combine the flour, baking soda, and salt in a bowl and set aside.

2. In the bowl of a stand mixer fitted with the paddle attachment, cream the butter on medium until light and fluffy, about 2 minutes. Add the peanut butter and beat for another 20 seconds on high. Add both sugars and cream for 1 minute on medium, scraping down the sides of the bowl as necessary.

3. Beat in the eggs one at a time, mixing well after each addition. Add the milk and vanilla extract and beat until just combined. Slowly add the flour mixture to the mixer bowl and beat until just incorporated. Wrap the dough in plastic and chill in the refrigerator for 1 hour.

4. Preheat the oven to 375°F. Line two baking sheets with parchment paper.

5. Remove the cookie dough from the refrigerator. Using a tablespoon measure, scoop small balls and place them 2 inches apart on the prepared baking sheets. Slightly flatten the balls with the tips of your fingers and sprinkle each cookie with a tiny pinch of fleur de sel.

6. Bake for 8 to 10 minutes, the let the cookies rest for 5 minutes on the baking sheet before transferring them to a wire rack to fully cool.

CLASSIC SPRITZ COOKIES

Cookies don't get much easier than this, and I'm sure that's why we always had what seemed like hundreds of these rich, buttery cookies around during the holidays. My grandmother, mother, and aunts all make spritz, a tradition shared by many Scandinavian immigrants. As a kid, I remember feeling these cookies were kind of ho-hum. They weren't the extravagant stained-glass masterpieces a friend's mom made every year, with jewel-like windows catching the light. Instead, these pressed cookies were only lightly adorned with colored sugars, or perhaps sprinkles, and they certainly didn't shimmer.

Recently I received a cookie press from my father-in-law with fourteen different design disks. I called my mother for her recipe, scribbling quickly while she dictated. Butter, sugar, vanilla. Yum. I whipped up a batch, and sure enough, they were delicious. I can now appreciate these light, dainty cookies for their taste and ease. To dress them up, though, and give them the holiday glitz they deserve, I sprinkle them with coarse sparkling sugar, so they too can shine.

MAKES ABOUT 6 DOZEN COOKIES

8 ounces (2 sticks) unsalted butter, at room temperature
2/3 cup granulated sugar
1/2 teaspoon salt
1 large egg plus 1 yolk, at room temperature
1 teaspoon pure vanilla extract
2 cups all-purpose flour
1/4 cup coarse sparkling sugar for decoration

1. Preheat the oven to 375°F. Line two baking sheets with parchment paper.

2. In the bowl of a stand mixer fitted with the paddle attachment, cream the butter, granulated sugar, and salt until light and fluffy, about 4 minutes. Add the egg, yolk, and vanilla extract. Beat until well mixed. Add the flour and mix on medium for about 45 seconds, until incorporated.

3. Press the dough through a cookie press 1 1/2 inches apart on a cookie sheet. (Or you can squeeze the cookies through a pastry bag using a star tip.) Sprinkle with the sparkling sugar.

4. Bake for 10 minutes, or until a pale golden brown. Let the cookies rest on the baking sheet for 5 minutes. Using a spatula, transfer to a wire rack to cool completely.

MORMOR'S ROSETTES

"It tastes like a deep-fried waffle," my daughter Camilla excitedly exclaimed the first time she tried a rosette, a crisp Norwegian cookie made by dipping a decorative cast-iron form into a thin batter and frying it. The cookies, which look impressive but are extremely easy to make ("Except for the fry mess," my mother always reminds me), slip right off the iron after less than half a minute of frying time. The iron is the primary component to this recipe. Without it, there is unfortunately no way to create these delicate cookies. I received my rosette maker from my *mormor* (literally mother's mother) but they are easily obtainable online and in stores around the holidays. Nordicware.com carries a great set (although they say theirs is Swedish—how dare they!). My grandmother always made these during December; now we make them on May 17 in recognition of Norway's national day, *Syttende Mai*.

MAKES ABOUT 3 DOZEN COOKIES

2 large eggs, at room temperature
1 tablespoon granulated sugar
1 cup milk
1 cup all-purpose flour
1/4 teaspoon salt
1 teaspoon pure vanilla extract
1 to 2 quarts vegetable oil
1/4 cup confectioners' sugar

1. Whisk the eggs in a bowl. Add the granulated sugar and continue to whisk. Stir in the milk. Add the flour and salt and whisk until combined. Add the vanilla extract and stir. The batter should be the same consistency as pancake batter.

2. Heat 2 to 3 inches of oil in a large pot to 365°F on a candy or deep-fry thermometer. Dip the iron into the oil for 2 minutes. Remove and drain the excess oil. Immediately dip the iron into the batter, not submerging the iron but just covering the sides with batter. Place the iron in the oil and fry until golden, about 30 seconds. It is important to keep the oil temperature at 365 to 370°F. If the oil gets too hot, the rosettes will stick to the iron. Gently use a fork or skewer to loosen the rosette from the iron and place on a paper towel–lined platter.

3. Continue to dip the iron and fry the batter. After all the batter is used, sift the confectioners' sugar evenly over the finished rosettes.

CLOUDBERRY KRUMKAKER CONES

Delicate, wafer-thin *krumkaker* cookies are made using a special iron or press. These golden rounds, a Norwegian specialty, resemble Italian pizzelles, but are slightly crisper and flavored with cardamom or vanilla—unlike the southern European variety, which usually tastes of anise or lemon. To make the cookies, the smallest amount of the egg batter is placed on a decoratively embossed iron, similar to a waffle iron, and cooked individually over the stovetop. Modern electric models are now available, but like my grandmother I stand over the stove and bake each cookie one at a time, over the burner. Seemingly fragile, these cookies are surprisingly pliable when warm, and may be rolled around a wooden form immediately after cooking to create a cone shape. They can be eaten plain, but I like to fill them with *multekrem* (cloudberry cream). A rare commodity, cloudberries look like a golden raspberry, and grow in sub-arctic regions. The unique flavor (not as sweet as a typical berry) is accompanied by a crunchy texture due to the berry's hard seeds. While available in Scandinavia, I've never seen a fresh cloudberry in the US, so I use cloudberry preserves (available from ingebretsens.com) to make *multekrem*. This recipe came from Marge Mjannes, who taught my grandmother to make these cookies, enabling her to continue a Norwegian tradition. *Takk skal du ha* (thanks so much), Marge.

**MAKES ABOUT 4 DOZEN
KRUMKAKER CONES**

2 large eggs, at room temperature

1 cup sugar

1 cup milk

1 teaspoon pure vanilla extract

1 1/2 cups all-purpose flour

1/4 teaspoon salt

8 tablespoons (1 stick) unsalted butter,
  melted

MULTEKREM

2 cups (1 pint) cold heavy cream

3 tablespoons confectioners' sugar

1/2 teaspoon pure vanilla extract

3/4 cup cloudberry preserves

1. Make the *krumkaker* cones: In a large bowl, using a whisk, beat the eggs and sugar until thick and pale yellow. Add the milk and stir until well combined. Stir in the vanilla extract. Add the flour and salt and stir until combined. Stir in the melted butter.

2. Gently spoon 1 teaspoon of batter onto the *krumkake* iron. Place the iron over medium heat on the stove top. Cook for 20 seconds on each side. While hot, roll immediately into a cone and place on a cookie sheet to cool. Continue with the remaining batter.

3. Make the *multekrem*: Using an electric mixer fitted with the whisk attachment, whip the cream until soft peaks form. Stir in the confectioners' sugar and vanilla extract. Fold in the preserves.

4. To serve, fill the *krumkaker* cones with the cloudberry whipped cream. Serve immediately or they become soft.

SKOLEBOLLER

Skoleboller, or school buns, truly are the ultimate Norwegian baked good and a favorite in our family. Some will argue that *skillingsboller* (cinnamon buns) are better, but of course there are also *sommerboller* (summer buns), *prinsesseboller* (princess buns—don't even go there!), and *rosinboller* (raisin buns), to name but a few more. Kids especially delight in these sweet rolls, which are eaten either in the morning, after school, or really most any time. I find them in Bergen's Baker Brun bakery, and each time I visit the shop, I like to think I'll try something new, but inevitably I leave with a *skolebolle*—a large, sweet yeast bun with crunchy coconut-covered edges surrounding a big bright-yellow circle of luscious custard. If you're a coconut-custard devotee like me, baked goods don't get much better than this.

MAKES SIXTEEN 4-INCH BUNS

DOUGH

1/4 cup warm water

1/2 cup plus 1 teaspoon sugar

1 envelope active dry yeast
  (2 1/4 teaspoons)

1 1/4 cups whole milk

4 tablespoons unsalted butter

2 teaspoons ground cardamom

1/2 teaspoon salt

4 cups all-purpose flour

CUSTARD FILLING

3 large egg yolks

1/3 cup sugar

2 tablespoons cornstarch

2 cups whole milk

1 teaspoon pure vanilla extract

COCONUT TOPPING

1/2 cup confectioners' sugar

2 tablespoons whole milk

3/4 cup finely shredded unsweetened
  coconut

1. Make the dough: If using a bread maker, place all the dough ingredients in a 1 1/2- to 2-pound bread maker according to the manufacturer's instructions with the following two changes: Melt the butter and add with the liquid ingredients and replace the 1/4 cup water with milk. Run the bread maker on the dough setting, and when it has finished its cycle turn the dough out onto a floured surface and skip ahead to step 6.

2. If you don't have a bread maker: Butter a large glass or ceramic bowl.

3. Pour the water in a bowl and add 1 teaspoon of the sugar. Stir to dissolve. Sprinkle the yeast over the water, stir again to dissolve, and let stand for 5 minutes, or until frothy.

4. Put the milk in a saucepan and cook over medium heat until it begins to steam and bubble slightly on the edges. Lower the heat and add the butter, the remaining 1/2 cup sugar, the cardamom, and salt. Stir until the butter is melted and the sugar is dissolved. Remove from the heat and let cool.

5. When the milk mixture has cooled, add the proofed yeast and stir. Add the flour and continue to stir until smooth. Turn the dough out onto a floured surface. Knead several times to form a soft dough. Sprinkle flour over the dough if it's sticky and knead a few more times. Place the dough in the prepared bowl and cover with a dishtowel. Set in a warm place to rise until doubled in size, about 1 hour.

6. Line two 11 x 17-inch baking sheets with parchment paper.

7. After the dough has risen, punch it down and turn it out onto a lightly floured surface. Divide the dough into 16 equal portions: Begin by dividing the entire dough ball into two halves. Then divide one of the portions in half again, and continue to

divide each portion into 4 more equal portions. Repeat with the second half of the dough. Form each of the 16 dough portions into round, flat buns (about 4 inches in diameter) and place 1 1/2 inches apart on the prepared baking sheets. Cover the buns with a dishtowel and let rise a second time, about 30 minutes.

8. Meanwhile, make the filling: In a heatproof bowl, whisk together the egg yolks, sugar, and cornstarch. Put the milk in a saucepan over medium-high heat and cook until it starts steaming and bubbling. Remove from the heat and slowly pour 1 cup of the heated milk in a thin stream into the egg mixture while constantly whisking. When smooth, gradually add the rest of the milk.

9. Pour the egg-milk mixture back into the saucepan and cook over medium-low heat until the mixture thickens and coats the back of a spoon, about 5 minutes, stirring constantly. Remove from the heat and let cool.

10. Preheat the oven to 350°F.

11. After the rolls have risen, use the bottom of a drinking glass (about 2 inches in diameter) dipped in flour to make a depression in the center of each bun. Fill each indentation with 1/8 cup of the cooked custard.

12. Bake for 12 to 14 minutes or until lightly golden on the edges. Remove from the oven and let cool.

13. While the buns are cooling, make the coconut topping: Stir together the confectioners' sugar and milk, whisking until smooth. Using a pastry brush, cover the sides of one cooled bun with the glaze and then sprinkle generously with coconut to cover the edges surrounding the custard. Continue glazing and sprinkling the buns one at a time to ensure the coconut adheres.

MOM'S BANANA CAKE

I fondly remember my mother having some type of foil-covered treat—brownies, cake, bars—in the kitchen at all times. Dreamy, creamy banana cake was often in the pan, the perfect after-school snack. This recipe takes a slight twist on traditional banana cake. The addition of oats gives the cake an almost nutty texture, making it denser than what a classic recipe may yield.

Use overripe bananas to ensure a fresh, banana flavor—even mushy bananas work. Hard bananas will not give flavor or contribute to the moist crumb. Serve this cake straight from the pan with a cup of tea—or better yet, a big glass of milk. You'll feel like you're sitting right at Mom's counter.

SERVES 12
BANANA CAKE

8 tablespoons (1 stick) unsalted butter, at room temperature

1 cup firmly packed light brown sugar

1/2 cup granulated sugar

2 large eggs, at room temperature

3/4 teaspoon baking soda

1/2 teaspoon baking powder

1/2 teaspoon salt

1/3 cup buttermilk or sour milk*

11/2 cups all-purpose flour

3/4 cup rolled oats

1 cup mashed bananas (2 to 3 very ripe)

* To make sour milk, add 1/2 teaspoon lemon juice to 1/3 cup whole milk and let stand for 5 minutes.

CREAM CHEESE FROSTING

8 tablespoons (1 stick) unsalted butter, at room temperature

One 8-ounce package cream cheese, at room temperature

2 cups confectioners' sugar

1 teaspoon pure vanilla extract

Dash of salt

1. Make the banana cake: Reheat the oven to 350°F. Grease a 13 x 9-inch baking pan using baking spray.

2. Cream the butter and sugars in the bowl of a stand mixer fitted with the paddle attachment for about 4 minutes on high, scraping down the sides of the bowl with a rubber spatula as necessary.

3. Add the eggs one at a time, blending each time until incorporated.

4. In a small bowl, dissolve the baking soda, baking powder, and salt into the sour milk. Alternately add the milk mixture and flour to the creamed butter mixture, starting and ending with the flour (add the flour in 1/2-cup increments), mixing to fully incorporate the ingredients each time.

5. Blend in the oats and mashed bananas. With the mixer on low, beat for 30 seconds.

6. Pour the batter into the prepared pan and bake for 20 to 25 minutes, until the top is golden and a toothpick inserted into the center of the cake comes out clean. Remove from the oven and let the cake cool completely in the pan.

7. Meanwhile, make the cream cheese frosting: In bowl of an electric mixer fitted with the paddle attachment, cream the butter and cream cheese for 2 minutes on high, scraping down the sides of the bowl with a rubber spatula as necessary. Sift the confectioners' sugar into the bowl and beat for another 2 minutes, or until smooth. Add the vanilla extract and salt and beat on high for another 30 seconds.

8. Using an offset spatula, frost the top of the cooled banana cake.

SPICED APPLE CIDER DOUGHNUTS

My eleven-year-old daughter, Anna, is a doughnut hound and I truly believe she comes by it genetically. I too am crazy for those fried cakes—and so were my forebears. When my grandmother was young in the early 1930s, she baked with *her* grandmother for a Women's Exchange in Madison, Wisconsin, frying upwards of 20 dozen doughnuts on Saturday mornings. This recipe, adapted from that one, involves several steps but is well worth the effort. I've added apples and cider to impart the taste of fall while bringing a favorite family tradition into our home, for Anna.

MAKES 20 DOUGHNUTS

DOUGHNUTS

1 cup sugar

3 large eggs, at room temperature

1/3 cup unsalted butter, melted

1/4 cup buttermilk

1/2 cup apple cider

1 teaspoon pure vanilla extract

4 cups all-purpose flour

4 teaspoons baking powder

2 teaspoons cinnamon

1/4 teaspoon nutmeg

1/8 teaspoon allspice

1/2 teaspoon salt

1 cup finely diced peeled apple, such as Honeycrisp or Gala

Vegetable oil for deep-frying

TOPPING

1 cup sugar

2 teaspoons cinnamon

1. Make the doughnuts: In the bowl of a stand mixer fitted with the paddle attachment, beat the sugar and eggs until thick and creamy. Add the butter and mix on low until fully incorporated.

2. Combine the buttermilk, cider, and vanilla extract in a small bowl. In a large bowl, combine the flour, baking powder, cinnamon, nutmeg, allspice, and salt. Alternately add the flour and buttermilk-cider mixture to the egg batter, beginning and ending with the flour. Combine thoroughly. Fold in the apple.

3. Turn the dough out onto a large piece of parchment or wax paper. Fold the paper over to cover the dough and place in the freezer for 30 minutes. The dough will be very sticky but will firm up while freezing.

4. Meanwhile, make the topping: Mix the sugar and cinnamon in a brown paper bag. Set aside.

5. In a large pot, start heating 3 to 4 inches of oil to 360°F, as measured by a candy or deep-fry thermometer. It will take about 15 minutes, and will be ready when your doughnuts are formed. If you'd rather wait, put your cut doughnuts in the refrigerator while waiting for the oil to heat.

6. On a lightly floured surface, roll out the firm dough to 1/2 inch thick. Cut 2 1/2-inch circles with 1-inch center holes (or use a doughnut cutter). The dough will be soft, which makes light, tender doughnuts when fried. Let the cut doughnuts rest for 5 minutes on a cookie sheet.

7. Fry 3 or 4 doughnuts at a time for about 1 1/2 minutes per side, or until golden brown. (Be sure to maintain the temperature of the oil, lowering or raising the heat accordingly, or the doughnuts will get hard instead of light and fluffy.

8. Shake the fried doughnuts in the cinnamon-sugar mixture. Serve warm.

GO-TO HOT FUDGE PUDDING CAKE

Warm chocolate pudding cake is one of the easiest desserts to make. No exaggeration, it mixes in one bowl and you can stir it up as your family is setting the table or as guests are walking in the door. Then you let it bake while you eat, with its inviting aroma wafting toward the table. This is one of those commit-this-to-memory recipes. Once you've gotten it down, you can whip it up anywhere. If you're a houseguest, offer to make pudding cake and your host will undoubtedly invite you back. But be sure to pack a little bag of good cocoa powder, because therein lies the secret: Use the very best cocoa you can get. Callebaut and Vahlrona, both available from numerous online sources, are two of my personal favorites. They cost a pretty penny though, so you may want to reserve them for special occasions. Other higher-end cocoas available at grocery stores, such as Droste or Ghiradelli, will still turn out a mighty fine product. With its crusty top and creamy, rich center, this cake is a modest cousin to today's trendy molten cakes. No need to be humble, though: Make it presentation-worthy. Mix and bake the dessert in a decorative crock or baking dish. And be sure to have some ice cream on hand to serve with it, a perfect pairing with the luscious hot fudge sauce.

SERVES 8

PUDDING CAKE

1 cup all-purpose flour

3/4 cup sugar

1/3 cup unsweetened cocoa powder, such as Callebaut

2 teaspoons baking powder

1/2 teaspoon salt

1/2 cup whole milk

1 tablespoon pure vanilla extract

2 tablespoons unsalted butter, melted

1/2 cup semisweet chocolate chips

TOPPING

2/3 cup firmly packed dark brown sugar

1/3 cup unsweetened cocoa powder, such as Callebaut

1 teaspoon instant espresso powder

1 3/4 cups boiling water

1. Make the pudding cake: Preheat the oven to 350°F. Grease an 8-inch square pan or a 2-quart casserole dish using baking spray.

2. In a bowl, combine the flour, sugar, cocoa powder, baking powder, and salt. Stir in the milk, vanilla extract, melted butter, and chocolate chips. The batter will be thick and difficult to stir but do your best to mix until smooth.

3. Using a rubber spatula, spread the mixture in the prepared pan; again, it will be very thick and may be difficult to spread but try to get it as even as possible.

4. Make the topping: Combine the brown sugar and cocoa powder in a bowl. Stir until the lumps disappear. Sprinkle the mixture evenly over the cake batter.

5. Dissolve the espresso powder into the boiling water and pour over the topping and batter.

6. Bake for 25 to 35 minutes. Do not overbake; a hot fudge sauce develops underneath the cakelike crust. Parts of the top should just be set with sauce bubbling out. The sauce will firm up after the cake has cooled a bit.

7. Serve warm over ice cream.

MILE-HIGH STRAWBERRY SHORTCAKE

Layers of buttery shortcake, juicy berries, and thick cream piled sky high are the epitome of a summer dessert, and the perfect finish to a family barbecue or Fourth of July picnic. Strawberry shortcake might just be the winner in our family for the most-served dessert during the past hundred years. Perhaps we make it often because of its ease, but the cake's irresistible combination of succulent fruit and generous amounts of cream make it an undeniable family favorite. More so, it looks as good as it tastes. The mouthwatering display, even more charming when slightly crooked, taunts us all through dinner until dessert is served—and we can finally dig in.

SERVES 10

SHORTCAKES

3 cups all-purpose flour

1 tablespoon plus 2 teaspoons baking powder

3 tablespoons sugar

1/2 teaspoon salt

14 tablespoons cold unsalted butter, cut into 1/2-inch pieces, plus 3 tablespoons melted

1 cup plus 2 tablespoons heavy cream

FILLING

1 quart plus 1 pint strawberries, hulled and sliced

1/4 cup granulated sugar

2 teaspoons lemon juice

1 quart heavy cream

1/4 cup confectioners' sugar

2 teaspoons pure vanilla extract

1. Make the shortcakes: Preheat oven to 425°F. Grease three 8-inch round cake pans with baking spray.

2. Stir together the flour, baking powder, sugar, and salt in a bowl. Sprinkle the butter pieces into the bowl. Using a pastry blender or two forks, work the butter into the dry ingredients until it's coarse and crumbly. Slowly add the cream, little by little, until a soft dough forms. Do not overstir.

3. Using your hands, form a large ball with the dough and then divide it into 3 parts. Press each section firmly and evenly into one of the prepared pans. Bake for 12 to 15 minutes, or until the tops become a very pale golden.

4. Meanwhile, make the filling: Put the strawberries in a bowl and toss with the granulated sugar and lemon juice. Remove half of the strawberries and lightly mash the remaining. Stir the whole strawberries back in and let stand for 30 minutes.

5. Remove the cakes from the oven. Let cool for 15 minutes before carefully removing them from the pans.

6. Meanwhile, in the bowl of an electric mixer fitted with the whisk attachment, whip the cream until thickened, but still soft. Stir in the confectioners' sugar and vanilla extract with a spoon.

7. Brush 1 tablespoon of the melted butter on the top of each cake with a pastry brush. Place one layer on a serving plate, butter side up. Spoon a third of the berries with their juice on top. Spread a thin layer of whipped cream over the berries. Top with a second cake layer. Spoon half of the remaining berries on top and another thin layer of cream. Repeat with the remaining cake layer and berries, reserving a few berries to decorate the top.

8. Dollop the remaining whipped cream on top of the cake and decorate with a few good-looking berries. Serve in wedges.

FRANGO MINT BROWNIES

A bite of a Frango mint takes me back to when I was six years old, walking down Chicago's State Street toward Marshal Field's with my family, exhilarated by the cold, the holiday windows, and the prospect of visiting the candy counter inside for a small square of creamy mint chocolate. Although Marshall Field's and Frango Mints are synonymous to some, the company did not actually create the candy but acquired production from Seattle's Frederick and Nelson department store in 1929. Marshall Field's was then bought by the May department store chain in 2004, and now Macy's distributes what was once Marshall Field's signature candy, still packaged in the familiar forest green rectangular box with white lettering.

Because Frangos are not so easily accessible, these brownies, loaded with the rich, thick candy, are a big treat in our house. They embody the essence of the Frango flavor (the perfect balance of chocolate and mint), while stretching it a little further. You get several chocolatey-minty bites instead of just one. While not all Macy's carry these delectable mints in-store, they are available online at macys.com. If you don't have access to Frangos, any mint-meltaway candy may be substituted (not Andes mints or Peppermint Patties, but a more chocolate-heavy mint).

MAKES 24 BROWNIES

8 tablespoons (1 stick) unsalted butter

3 ounces unsweetened chocolate

2 large eggs, at room temperature

1 cup sugar

1 teaspoon pure vanilla extract

1/2 cup plus 2 tablespoons all-purpose flour

1/8 teaspoon salt

3/4 cup chopped Frango Mints (about 4 ounces)

1. Preheat the oven to 350°F. Line an 8-inch square baking pan with parchment paper, leaving a 1-inch overhang on two sides. Grease the pan with baking spray.

2. Melt the butter and unsweetened chocolate together in a small saucepan over low heat. Set aside to cool.

3. In a large bowl, whisk together the eggs, sugar, and vanilla extract until thoroughly combined and slightly thickened, about 100 strokes.

4. Whisk in the cooled chocolate-butter mixture. Stir in the flour and salt until just combined. Do not overmix. Gently stir in the chopped Frango mints.

5. Spread the batter in the prepared pan, using a rubber spatula to distribute it evenly, and bake for 20 to 25 minutes or until a toothpick inserted into the brownies comes out with a few moist crumbs attached.

6. It is important to let the brownies cool in the pan for 1 hour before cutting. This allows the brownies to set. Cut into 1 1/2 x 2-inch rectangles and serve.

PEACHES-IN-A-POCKET WITH WARM VANILLA SAUCE

Tender, sweet dough gathered around warm, juicy peaches smothered in vanilla pudding sauce. One of my mother's favored desserts from childhood, this recipe is her summer standard. She makes it often during peach season, and swaps between making one big cake (she divides the dough in half, forms two 9-inch circles, places one circle in the bottom of a 9-inch pan, covers it with peaches, and places the second dough circle on top) and individual serving sizes. The dough surrounding the peaches becomes almost custardy when baked. For some, the sauce—a super-sweet butter sauce—may be overkill, but it's what my mother and grandmother always serve with this peach dessert that they call Peach Pudding (even though these bundles don't resemble pudding at all, hence my name change).

SERVES 8
PEACHES-IN-A-POCKET

$3^1/2$ cups thinly sliced peeled peaches (about $1^1/2$ pounds)

$1/4$ cup plus 2 teaspoons granulated sugar

1 tablespoon lemon juice

2 cups all-purpose flour

1 tablespoon baking powder

1 teaspoon salt

$1^1/2$ cups heavy cream

2 tablespoons unsalted butter, melted

VANILLA PUDDING SAUCE

$1/3$ cup sugar

1 tablespoon cornstarch

$1/3$ cup water

$1^1/2$ tablepoons unsalted butter

$1/2$ teaspoon pure vanilla extract

Pinch of salt

1. Make the peaches-in-a-pocket: Preheat oven to 400°F. Line a baking sheet with parchment paper.

2. Toss the peaches, $1/4$ cup of the sugar, and the lemon juice together in a bowl. Set aside.

3. Stir together the flour, baking powder, and salt in another bowl. Add the cream and stir well. The dough will be sticky.

4. Turn the dough out onto a lightly floured surface and form into an 8 x 16-inch rectangle. Cut into eight 4-inch squares. Place about $1/4$ cup sliced peaches in the center of each square. Bring all four corners of a dough square to the top and pinch together, making a pocket around the peaches. Repeat with all the squares.

5. Using a pastry brush, coat each pocket with melted butter. Sprinkle lightly with the remaining 2 teaspoons sugar. Bake for 20 to 25 minutes, or until lightly golden.

6. Meanwhile, make the vanilla pudding sauce: Stir together the sugar and cornstarch in a small saucepan. Add the water and simmer over medium heat until thickened. (If it becomes too thick, add a little more water.)

7. Remove from the heat and stir in the butter, vanilla extract, and salt. Pour into a serving carafe and serve immediately with the peaches-in-a-pocket.

COOKIES-AND-CREAM ICE CREAM

One of the country's bestselling ice cream flavors in the 1980s, cookies-and-cream ice cream, also referred to as "cookies 'n cream," is as iconic to that decade as shoulder pads and big hair. Unlike those fads, a smooth vanilla ice cream loaded with chunks of Oreos—another American favorite—has proven to have staying power. In the 1980s, with big hair myself, I pulled our never-been-opened ice cream maker out from the basement. It was not a fancy electric one, but a hand-crank, salt-and-ice type. As my parents had grounded me and I needed something to do, I decided to make ice cream, much to my mother's chagrin (remember, she doesn't like messes). What should have taken an hour or two turned into a day-long project requiring bags of ice and boxes of rock salt. The kitchen was covered with smashed cookies and pools of water and cream. While I managed to create a darn good ice cream, I got something better: freedom. My mother said, "Your punishment is over, go find something else to do."

MAKES 1 QUART

1 cup whole milk

2 cups heavy cream

3/4 cup sugar

2 teaspoons pure vanilla extract

1 1/2 cups crushed chocolate sandwich cookies such as Newman's Os or Oreos (about 15 cookies)

1. Put the milk, cream, and sugar in a heavy saucepan over medium heat and cook until the sugar is dissolved and the mixture starts to steam and come to a slight simmer, about 5 minutes.

2. Remove from the heat and stir in the vanilla extract. Cool to room temperature, then chill for at least 4 hours or overnight in the refrigerator.

3. Freeze the cooled mixture in an ice cream maker, according to the manufacturer's directions. When the ice cream maker has completed its cycle, place the ice cream in a large bowl and gently fold in the crushed cookies. Move the ice cream to a freezer-safe container and freeze for at least 1 hour before serving.

JAMAICAN SWEET POTATO PUDDING

Nutmeg is a key flavor in many Jamaican dishes, including this dessert, which is one of my father-in-law David's favorites from childhood. On our most recent trip to Jamaica, we met Oliver Bailey at his restaurant, Oliver's Dutch Pot, in Treasure Beach. Oliver kindly offered to teach us to make sweet potato pudding "the traditional way," as he said, "with ´ell on top, ´ell on bottom." I must have asked him to repeat himself three times before David interjected with a translation: hell on top, hell on bottom. Oliver explained that we would cook it the traditional way, over an outdoor fire with coals on top and bottom, hence the expression. Anna, Camilla, and I peeled and grated white sweet potatoes, grated nutmeg, and watched as Oliver added coconut milk, flour, sugar, and a few other choice ingredients. We poured the mixture into a large Dutch oven that began to bake over the fire at about quarter past five. While it cooked, we dined on curried goat, coconut shrimp, jerk chicken, and rice and peas. As the sun set, the fire glowed while the "hallelujah" formed (that's what they call the creamy part that develops on the top of pudding, between the ´ell on top, ´ell on bottom). After three hours, the center was set and the pudding was ready. Now was our chance to taste what had been permeating the air with its sweet nutmeg perfume. It tasted just as the smell promised—sublime.

SERVES 10 TO 12

2 pounds (about 4 to 5) sweet potatoes, peeled and finely grated*

3/4 cup all-purpose flour

2 tablespoons cornmeal

3/4 cups firmly packed light brown sugar

1 tablespoon freshly grated nutmeg

1 teaspoon salt

2 1/2 cups coconut milk

6 ounces evaporated milk

3 tablespoons unsalted butter, melted

1 tablespoon pure vanilla extract

* It is key to grate these potatoes as finely as possible. They will have very little texture after being grated. When you rub the grated potatoes between your fingers, they should feel soft.

1. Preheat the oven to 350°F. Grease a 9-inch round springform pan with baking spray. Wrap the outside of the pan with aluminum foil to prevent any leaking. Place on a baking sheet.

2. In a 4- to 5-quart bowl, thoroughly stir together the sweet potatoes, flour, cornmeal, brown sugar, nutmeg, and salt.

3. In a second bowl, whisk together the coconut and evaporated milks, the butter, and vanilla. Add this liquid mixture to the sweet potatoes and stir thoroughly until smooth. This will seem like a tremendous amount of liquid, but it fits in the 9-inch pan.

4. Pour the mixture into the prepared pan.

5. Bake for 1 1/2 to 2 1/2 hours, or until a knife inserted into the center of the pudding comes out clean. Increase the temperature to 400°F if needed after 2 hours of baking. Remove from the oven and after it has cooled, chill in the refrigerator overnight. Cut into wedges and serve chilled or at room temperature.

NILLA WAFER PUDDING

Pudding was an easy after-school snack when I was growing up. It was one of the first things I learned to cook, along with instant Cream of Wheat and cinnamon toast. One of my favorite recipe creations was vanilla pudding, bananas, and crushed Nilla Wafers. I would scoop it in a glass and stir in my toppings. (Later I learned that bananas and Nilla Wafers work well with ice cream in a blender too.) A little more time intensive than the Jell-O cook-and-serve packs of my childhood, this recipe for Nilla Wafer Pudding satisfies my sentimental side, while improving on history with a homemade pudding that's light, luscious, and pure. The yield is large enough to serve a crowd of kids or dish out at a backyard barbecue. For a more elegant presentation, assemble in a trifle bowl.

SERVES 10 TO 12

3 large egg yolks
3/4 cup granulated sugar
3 tablespoons cornstarch
1/2 teaspoon salt
3 cups whole milk
2 tablespoons unsalted butter
1 teaspoon pure vanilla extract
1 cup (1/2 pint) cold heavy cream
1/4 cup confectioners' sugar
4 ripe bananas
1 tablespoon lemon juice
50 vanilla wafers, crushed, plus a few
    whole for decoration

1. Put the egg yolks in a heatproof bowl and whisk slightly. Set aside.

2. Combine the sugar, cornstarch, and salt in a medium saucepan over medium heat. Carefully add the milk to the pan, whisking constantly for 8 minutes or until the mixture starts to thicken. Do not let the pudding come to a complete full boil, just a gentle one.

3. Remove the pan from the heat and pour half the thickened milk into the egg yolks and whisk well.

4. Return the to the heat. Gently add the yolk mixture to the pan. While stirring constantly, bring the mixture back to a gentle boil, and continue to stir for 1 more minute.

5. Remove from the heat and stir in the butter and ½ teaspoon of the vanilla extract. Set aside.

6. Whip the cream until light and fluffy. Do not overbeat. Stir in the confectioners' sugar and remaining 1/2 teaspoon vanilla extract.

7. Cut the bananas into 1/2-inch slices and sprinkle with the lemon juice. Carefully toss to coat all the bananas.

8. In the bottom of a 2-quart bowl, spoon in 2 cups of the vanilla pudding. Sprinkle with 1/2 cup crushed wafers. Arrange 1 cup of the sliced bananas decoratively over the wafers. Spoon in the rest of the pudding and coat with 1 cup crushed wafers. Arrange the remaining bananas (reserve a few slices for decoration) on top of the wafers. Cover the entire surface with the whipped cream. Decorate with the reserved banana slices and whole wafers. Serve immediately or put in the refrigerator until ready to serve.

LISA'S LEMON MUFFINS

My sister and brother-in-law's house in the Chicago suburbs is the epicenter for our extended family, a place where all the relatives from Wisconsin, Michigan, Illinois, and farther afield congregate. A hostess by nature, my sister Lisa welcomes everyone. When the house is full of guests, you'll find two fridges and a freezer full of food, several types of soup on the stovetop, and meals aplenty. It's such a pleasure waking up to freshly brewed coffee and a large breakfast comprised of many dishes: the mandatory Midwestern egg bake, sausages, bacon, fruit, and always some type of muffin or bread. This lemon muffin recipe is hers, one that she has served to many guests. I've added raspberries for a fresh zing, as they give a deep intensity to the flavor, even though Lisa herself despises fruit in muffins. But isn't that my job as the consummate little sister to provoke?

MAKES 12 MUFFINS

MUFFINS

1 cup all-purpose flour
1 cup ground rolled oats*
$2/3$ cup sugar
2 teaspoons baking powder
$1/2$ teaspoon salt
1 large egg, lightly beaten
$2/3$ cup milk
1 tablespoon grated lemon zest
1 tablespoon lemon juice
1 teaspoon pure vanilla extract
$1/3$ cup vegetable oil
$11/2$ cups fresh red raspberries

* Put the oats in a blender or food processor and run the machine until they are ground to an almost flourlike texture.

GLAZE

$3/4$ cup confectioners' sugar
3 tablespoons lemon juice
1 teaspoon grated lemon zest
1 tablespoon lemon curd (optional)

1. Make the muffins: Preheat the oven to 400°F. Line a standard 12-cup muffin pan with paper liners.

2. In a large bowl, combine the flour, oats, sugar, baking powder, and salt. Add the egg, milk, zest, lemon juice, vanilla extract, and oil and stir until thoroughly combined. Do not overmix, as it will make the muffins tough. Gently fold in the raspberries.

3. Divide the batter among the 12 prepared muffin cups, which will be almost filled to the top with batter. Bake for 15 to 18 minutes, until a toothpick inserted in the center of a muffin comes out clean. The tops will not brown.

4. Meanwhile, make the glaze: Whisk together the confectioners' sugar and lemon juice in a small saucepan and stir over medium heat until the mixture just starts to bubble.

5. Remove from the heat and stir in the zest and curd, if using. Let cool for 2 minutes.

6. Place the muffins on a cooling rack set over wax paper. Drizzle 1 teaspoon glaze over each muffin.

CRISS-CROSS COFFEE CAKE

During my childhood summers, my cousin Jenny and I would stay parentless for a week with our grandparents or aunt and uncle. At my aunt Susie's, we partook in woodworking. An avid craftswoman, she taught us how to sand with the grain and the difference between a jigsaw and band saw. By the end of the week, we had proudly created several stunning projects to take home. My grandmother's activity time took place in the kitchen. We learned to make cookies, yeast rolls, and, my favorite, apricot coffee cake. My mother shied away from yeast, so anything that required rising was a mystery to me. My grandmother, on the other hand, proofed, kneaded, and formed the dough so adeptly it was as if she were simply brushing her teeth. I learned a lot on those summer days, although I'm still aiming to create that bakery-like finish my grandmother achieves.

SERVES 10
DOUGH

1/4 cup very warm water

1/4 cup plus 1 teaspoon sugar

1 envelope active dry yeast
  (2 1/4 teaspoons)

1/3 cup whole milk

1/3 cup plus 2 tablespoons unsalted
  butter, at room temperature

3/4 teaspoon plus a pinch of salt

1 large egg, lightly beaten

2 1/2 cups all-purpose flour

1/2 cup orange-apricot marmalade*

1/4 teaspoon freshly grated nutmeg

3 1/2 tablespoons unsalted butter,
  at room temperature

1/4 cup chopped pecans (optional)

* My favorite brand is Sarabeth's.
  You may use any type of preserve
  or marmalade in this coffeecake,
  just omit the nutmeg.

1. If you're using a bread maker, place all the ingredients in a 1 1/2- to 2-pound bread maker according to the manufacturer's instructions with the following two changes: Melt the butter and add with the liquid ingredients; replace the 1/4 cup water with milk. Run the machine on the dough setting and when finished, turn it out onto a floured surface and skip ahead to step 8.

2. If not using a bread maker, butter a large glass or ceramic bowl.

3. To proof the yeast, put the water in a bowl and add 1 teaspoon of the sugar. Stir to dissolve. Sprinkle the yeast over the water, stir again to dissolve, and let stand for 5 minutes, or until frothy.

4. Put the milk in a saucepan and cook over medium heat until it begins to steam and bubble slightly on the edges. Lower the heat and add the 1/3 cup butter, 1/4 cup sugar, and 3/4 teaspoons of the salt. Stir until the butter is melted and the sugar is dissolved. Remove from the heat and let cool.

5. Meanwhile, lightly beat the egg in a liquid measuring cup. Add enough water to make 3/4 cup total.

6. When the milk mixture has cooled, add the proofed yeast and egg mixture and stir. Add the flour and continue to stir until smooth. The dough should be stiff. Turn the dough out onto a floured surface.

GLAZE

1/2 cup confectioners' sugar
1 tablespoon milk
1/4 teaspoon pure vanilla extract

7. Knead several times to form a soft dough. Sprinkle flour over the dough if it's sticky and knead a few more times. Place the dough in the prepared bowl and cover with a dishtowel. Set in a warm place to rise until doubled in size, about 1 hour.

8. Line an 11 x 17-inch baking sheet with parchment paper. Stir together the marmalade, nutmeg, and a pinch of salt in a small bowl and set aside.

9. After the dough has risen, punch it down and turn it out onto a lightly floured surface. Knead 2 tablespoons softened butter into the dough. Form the dough into an 11- x 17-inch rectangle about 1/4 inch thick (you may want to do this on parchment on the counter or directly on the parchment on the baking pan; the coffee cake is hard to move once assembled).

10. Spread the remaining 1 1/2 tablespoons softened butter gently over the dough. Spoon the reserved marmalade filling on the center third of the dough and sprinkle with the nuts, if using. Cut 9 slits in each of the two side portions, beginning on the short ends up to the filling. Alternately fold the dough strips toward the center of the filling, criss-crossing each strip as you go along. Cover the coffee cake with a dishtowel and let rise a second time, for about 1 hour.

11. Preheat the oven to 350°F.

12. Bake the risen coffee cake for 30 minutes, or until browned.

13. Meanwhile, make the glaze: In a small bowl, whisk together the confectioners' sugar, milk, and vanilla extract. Using a spoon, drizzle the glaze back and forth over the baked coffee cake.

CELEBRATING

Our most treasured family heirlooms
are our sweet family moments.

UNKNOWN

There is no question that food defines important moments in my family life—holidays, birthdays, weddings. My husband and I still have a piece of our wedding cake stashed in the back of our freezer. I just can't bear to get rid of it. We were married in the fall in New York's Adirondack mountains. The memory of the three-tiered apple spice cake with colorful fondant leaves, so representative of the place and time, will always live with me.

Recipes bear so much weight. But sometimes the memory is better than the reality. "Was this really the cake Nonna used to make? It tastes so different." And it's not always because the recipe execution went awry. It's akin to walking into your childhood home after not being there for thirty years. "Wow, it always seemed so much grander," some will say. While some recipes may disappoint, others will stand the test of time. It's those recipes you want to preserve.

A familiar food or baked good has the power to make you feel in a comfortable place, to evoke an emotional response. I feel a nostalgic bliss when I bite into a gooey-sticky German's Chocolate Cake, my birthday cake of choice. A bite of Angel Food Cake and I envision my mother (not because she's an angel—although she is—but because it's her favorite cake!). The list goes on and on.

It's important to document favorite recipes. Use them to carry on—or create—celebratory traditions. When a child is welcomed on his birthday morn with a festive table set with favored treats, he'll feel loved and honored. When he knows he'll receive that same welcome every year, he'll appreciate the tradition, the continued love, and the strong bond of family.

Of course, Thanksgiving, Christmas, Hanukkah, Easter, Passover, and the other various holidays have their share of fond food remembrances, and the recipes you use should be archived. But don't forget the everyday occurrences worth celebrating: a job promotion, a new pet, a good grade, a soccer goal, a ballet recital, even the daffodils coming up!

Those are the moments that deserve a cake, a tart, or a pie. Conversation and laughter will be exchanged while sharing that special food, and while the conversation is something you'll be able to document only in your mind, that same baked treat can be recreated and may remind you of those happy times for years to come.

10 WAYS TO MAKE SMALL MOMENTS BIG

1. IT'S ALL ABOUT THE CAKE STAND Cake stands have a way of raising desserts to another level. And the dessert need not be a cake. Piles of cookies or doughnuts look elegant when elevated above the rest of the table. Inexpensive cake stands can be found at department stores and cooking supply stores. Second-hand stores and junk shops are great places to find vintage ones. Even the most basic stand can be dressed up with a paper garland. A table decked out with multiple, mismatched cake stands is pure eye candy.

2. HANG A CLOTH BANNER Bedazzling the dining room with balloons and streamers is a must for every birthday celebrated in our house. We also have a stash of tissue-paper flowers and a felt birthday banner. Create your own pennant banner and consider adding a new flag for each occasion it's hung.

3. USE A CANDLE RING Originally a German tradition, using birthday candle rings are a festive way to honor a child's birthday. The ring, which is usually made of wood, has twelve holes with 12 decorative wooden placeholders. Beginning with your child's first birthday, you replace one placeholder with a candle. Your child will look forward to adding a candle each year, and hopefully doing the same with his or her children and grandchildren. Thewoodenwagon.com sells rings with a large selection of decorative placeholders.

4. GIFT A PLATE A YEAR Giving the same type of gift annually is a wonderful way to mark holidays and birthdays. I know someone who inherited a collection of 18 silver plates, each one given to her grandmother on her birthday, from her first to her eighteenth. Christmas, Passover, and other holidays are also special times to commemorate with different types of dessert plates, from hand-painted china to Depression glass.

5. MAKE BREAKFAST A CROWNING OCCASION There's nothing like waking up to a celebratory breakfast highlighting a momentous occasion, whether it's a birthday or the first day of a new job. Bake a favorite breakfast treat and create a crown that is used for such times. It'll make the honoree feel regal.

6. USE FRESH FLOWERS AND PIPED FROSTING A small batch of colored buttercream piped from a baggie and colorful, fresh flowers can turn any dessert into a show-stopping centerpiece. Use frosting to pipe letters or numbers on any type of baked good. No need to make frosting flowers, though. Use real roses, violets, lavender, impatiens, pansies, daisies, or other non-toxic blossoms to dress up a cake or cupcakes (try to get flowers that are organically grown and not sprayed with pesticides).

7. DESIGN A PHOTO ALBUM WITH RECIPES Start an album dedicated solely to a special holiday or birthday. Document the people, the food, the discussions, and include photos and recipes used on that day.

8. HOST A BAKING PARTY Invite family and friends over to bake a favorite recipe with you. Labor-intensive recipes like rugelach are more fun to make with the help of others. Ask guests to bring their heirloom recipes.

9. CREATE A TIME CAPSULE IN A JAR Collect memorabilia marking a special occasion, and be sure to include a recipe that was used on that day. Carefully place the items in a large glass jar, seal the cap, and set the jar on a shelf, labeled with the year in which the capsule may be opened by future family members.

10. LAMINATE PHOTO CAKE CARDS Every year, take a photo of family members with their birthday cakes. Print the photo out in a 3 x 5-inch format, tag it with the year, laminate it, and mount it on a stick. Use the cards to decorate future birthday cakes, which will serve as sweet reminders of birthdays past.

SPOOKTACULAR CHEESECAKE ⧗

Velvety and rich, cheesecake has always been near and dear to my heart. It was one of the first grown-up desserts I learned to make, straight from the pages of Rosso and Lukins's *The New Basics Cookbook*. I served the book's Almond Sour Cream Cheesecake at more dinner parties than I care to count, but it always received rave reviews. A little cheesecaked-out, I stopped making them for a while. My daughter Camilla shares the same fondness I have for the indulgent cake, and for a Halloween party inspired me to reignite my passion. The chocolatey web that dons the top of this cheesecake is easy to create but makes a spectacular presentation. Add a few toy spiders for an even more frightening display. The recipe for this pure, undoctored cheesecake is adapted from that *New Basics* favorite of mine.

SERVES 10 TO 12

CRUST

$1/2$ cup slivered almonds

2 cups ground chocolate wafer cookies

$1/4$ cup sugar

8 tablespoons (1 stick) unsalted butter, melted

FILLING

Three 8-ounce packages cream cheese, at room temperature

$1/2$ cup sugar

1 teaspoon lemon juice

1 teaspoon pure vanilla extract

1 teaspoon pure almond extract

3 large eggs, at room temperature

TOPPING

1 cup sour cream

1 tablespoon sugar

$1/4$ cup bittersweet chocolate chips

2 tablespoons unsalted butter

1. Preheat the oven to 375°F.

2. Make the crust: Using a food processor, finely grind the almonds. Add the cookies, sugar, and melted butter and pulse until thoroughly combined. Firmly press the cookie mixture into the bottom of a 9-inch springform pan, continuing to form the crust halfway up the sides of the pan. Set aside.

3. Make the filling: Combine the cream cheese, sugar, lemon juice, and vanilla and almond extracts in a food processor. When well blended, add the eggs and process until thoroughly combined. Pour the filling into the prepared pan with the crust and bake for 45 to 50 minutes.

4. Meanwhile, start the topping: Combine the sour cream and sugar in a small bowl.

5. When the cake has just begun to crack, remove it from the oven and lower the oven temperature to 350°F. Spread the topping evenly over the cake and bake for 7 to 10 minutes, or until the topping is set. Remove from the oven and let the cake cool for 1 hour before decorating.

6. In a small saucepan over medium heat, melt the chocolate chips and butter together, stirring constantly. Remove from the heat and allow the chocolate to cool before placing it in a plastic resealable bag. Cut a small corner off one side. Twist the top of the bag slightly and gently squeeze out the chocolate onto a piece of wax paper. Practice making a small circle.

7. Starting in the center of the cake, make a circle. Continue making concentric circles around the first circle until you've covered the entire cake with circles. Next, slowly drag a toothpick from the center of the cake to the outside edge moving in a straight line the entire way. Move your way around the cake, dragging the toothpick to the outer edge 8 to 10 times. Refrigerate the cake for at least 2 hours before serving.

DEVILICOUS CHOCOLATE MARSHMALLOW CUPCAKES

My friend Jenny Bella runs a small baking business from her home and specializes in cupcakes—she has baked hundreds of them to perfect her recipes. This particular one she developed mimics a Hostess cupcake (but is oh-so-much better). The rich, moist chocolate crumb is complemented by a creamy vanilla filling. When Jenny decorates the smooth, glossy ganache, she pipes out a vanilla swirly heart instead of the signature Hostess squiggle. I've ditched the swirls and squiggles altogether and made these cupcakes devilish, using pieces of candy—licorice, candy corn, jelly beans, and pastilles—to create ghoulish characters that are sinfully sweet, and the perfect Halloween treat!

MAKES 24 CUPCAKES

CUPCAKES

2 cups all-purpose flour

6 tablespoons unsweetened cocoa powder

2 cups sugar

2 teaspoons baking soda

1 teaspoon salt

1/2 cup canola oil

2 large eggs, lightly beaten

1 1/2 cups strong brewed coffee, cooled

1 teaspoon pure vanilla extract

VANILLA FILLING

8 tablespoons (1 stick) unsalted butter, at room temperature

2 cups sifted confectioners' sugar

1 tablespoon heavy cream

1/4 teaspoon pure vanilla extract

GANACHE

1/2 cup Ghiradelli 60% cacao bittersweet chocolate chips

1/2 cup heavy cream

TOPPING

Assorted candy such as licorice, jelly beans, and pastilles

1/2 cup heavy cream

1. Preheat the oven to 375°F. Line two standard cupcake pans with paper liners.

2. Whisk the flour, cocoa powder, sugar, baking soda, and salt together in a large bowl. Add the oil, eggs, coffee, and vanilla extract and stir thoroughly for 2 minutes, stopping and scraping down the sides of the bowl with a rubber spatula as neccesary. The batter will be somewhat liquidy.

3. Fill the cupcake liners two-thirds full with batter and bake for 30 minutes, or until a toothpick inserted into the center of a cupcake comes out with a few moist crumbs attached. Let cool on a wire rack.

4. Meanwhile, make the vanilla filling: Combine the butter, confectioners' sugar, cream, and vanilla extract in the bowl of an electric mixer fitted with the whisk attachment. Beat on high for 3 minutes or until light and fluffy. Set aside.

5. Make the ganache: Heat the cream in a small pan until it steams and tiny bubbles start to form on the edges of the pan. Remove from the heat and stir in the chocolate chips until smooth and glossy.

6. To assemble the cupcakes, fill a decorating press fitted with a filling tip (similar to a cookie press) or a pastry bag with a round tip with the vanilla filling. Gently push the tip of the press into each cupcake and squeeze until you feel the pressure of the filling against the tip.

7. Dip the top of each filled cupcake into the ganache, remove, and let set. Use the assorted candy to decorate the top of each cupcake with a devilish face.

PEAR CRANBERRY CRUMB TART

Pumpkin pie is a given for every Thanksgiving spent with my family; there will be one, if not two or three, pumpkin pies made following the instructions straight off the back of a Libby's Pure Pumpkin can. Don't get me wrong, the recipe yields a tasty pie, but I enjoy variety. I like to have a few other desserts, including this Pear Cranberry Crumb Tart, on the dessert table. Tart cherries, pears, and cranberries tossed with ginger, cinnamon, and a slight hint of orange make a bright, zesty combination—the perfect complement to a predictable yet essential pumpkin pie. After all, Thanksgiving is all about bounty.

SERVES 8

CRUST

1 1/4 cups all-purpose flour

1/2 teaspoon salt

3 tablespoons sugar

12 tablespoons (1 1/2 sticks) cold unsalted
   butter, cut into 1-inch chunks

2 tablespoons water

1 large egg yolk

FILLING

1 cup fresh cranberries

3/4 cup sugar

1 teaspoon orange zest

3 tablespoons orange juice

1 1/2 teaspoons grated fresh ginger

1/4 teaspoon ground cinnamon

1/2 cup dried cherries

2 pears, peeled and sliced (about 1 1/2 cups)

1/4 cup cranberry chutney, such as
   Crosse and Blackwell brand

1 tablespoon all-purpose flour

2 tablespoons cornstarch

TOPPING

1/4 cup all-purpose flour

3 tablespoons light brown sugar

1/4 teaspoon salt

3 tablespoons cold unsalted butter,
   cut into 1/2-inch chunks

1. Make the crust: In a bowl, stir together the flour, salt, and sugar.

2. Put the butter chunks in the bowl with the flour mixture. Using a pastry blender, work the butter into the dry ingredients until coarse crumbs form.

3. Whisk together the water and egg yolk and slowly add to the flour-butter mixture, stirring until moist clumps appear.

4. Gather the dough into a ball and press evenly into a 9-inch removable-bottom tart pan. Put the crust in the freezer while you prepare the filling.

5. Preheat the oven to 350°F.

6. Make the filling: Put 1/2 cup of the cranberries, the sugar, orange zest, orange juice, ginger, and cinnamon in the bowl of a food processor. Pulse 6 to 8 times, or until the cranberries are roughly chopped. Transfer to a large bowl and add the remaining cranberries, the dried cherries, pears, and chutney. Add the flour and cornstarch and toss well. Set aside.

7. Make the topping: Stir together the flour, brown sugar, and salt in a bowl. Add the butter chunks and mash together with a fork. Using your fingers, make some clumps in the mixture.

8. Remove the crust from the freezer and spoon in the filling. Sprinkle the topping evenly over the entire crust.

9. Place the tart pan on a foil-lined baking sheet and bake for 50 minutes, or until bubbling and golden. Remove the tart from the oven and let cool for about 10 minutes before removing the outer ring. Cool completely before serving.

SUPER-EASY SUGAR COOKIES

I used to think making cut-out cookies was a chore. I disliked the struggle of rolling out a hard, refrigerated lump of dough. Then Robin Chess, who teaches kids' cooking classes at our local elementary school, showed me how she effortlessly makes hundreds of cut-out cookies every holiday season with her students, ages five to eight. Straight from the mixing bowl, she places small handfuls of dough between two sheets of wax paper and has the kids roll it out, no sticking, no struggle. When she makes these cookies, they go right into the oven—no chilling necessary—to avoid waiting time. For a slightly crisper cookie, I refrigerate them for 20 minutes on the baking sheets after they've been cut. If you're in a rush, though, this step is not essential to a tasty cookie. Ease rules in this recipe, which yields a not-too-sweet, not-too-thick, classic crisp-on-the-edges sugar cookie.

MAKES 40 COOKIES

SUGAR COOKIES

8 ounces (2 sticks) unsalted butter, at room temperature

1 cup sugar

1 large egg, at room temperature

1 teaspoon pure vanilla extract

3 cups all-purpose flour

2 teaspoons baking powder

1/2 teaspoon salt

ROYAL ICING

2 large egg whites

4 cups confectioners' sugar

1 teaspoon pure vanilla extract

1 tablespoon lemon juice

Food coloring (optional)

TOPPINGS (OPTIONAL)

Colored sugars

Sprinkles

Dragees

1. Preheat the oven to 375°F. Line two cookie sheets with parchment paper.

2. Put the butter in the bowl of a stand mixer fitted with the paddle attachment and beat on medium for 2 minutes. Add the sugar and beat on medium for another 2 minutes, scraping down the sides of the bowl as necessary.

3. Add the egg and vanilla extract to the bowl and continue to beat on medium for another 30 seconds. Add the flour, baking powder, and salt and beat on low to medium for $1^1/2$ to 2 minutes, or until the dough comes together to form a ball.

4. Turn the dough out onto a lightly floured surface. Divide into two equal portions. Working with one portion at a time, roll the dough out to ¼ inch thick. Cut the dough using cookie cutters and gently lift the shapes with a spatula and place on the prepared cookie sheet. Refrigerate on the sheets for 20 minutes.

5. Remove the cookies from the refrigerator and bake for 8 minutes, or until golden brown on the edges. Let cool on the baking sheet for 10 minutes before transferring to a wire rack to cool completely.

6. Meanwhile, make the royal icing: In the bowl of a stand mixer fitted with the whisk attachment, beat the egg whites until soft peaks form. Sift the confectioners' sugar into the bowl. Beat for another minute or two. The icing should be somewhat stiff (spreadable but not so thin it will run off the edges of the cookie). Stir in the vanilla extract and lemon juice.

7. If desired, divide the icing among several bowls and color using food coloring. Cover the top of the icing with a damp paper towel to prevent it from drying out until using.

8. Decorate the cooled cookies with the royal icing, colored sugars, sprinkles, and/or dragees.

NORWEGIAN PEPPERKAKER (GINGER COOKIES)

The heavy darkness of the Norwegian winter is magically lifted during *Jultid* (Christmastime). As if enchanted dust had been sprinkled over the country, twinkling lights appear, glögg simmers on stovetops, and holiday treats are baked.

Distinctly thin and crisp, *pepperkaker* (thin ginger cookies) are the quintessential Norwegian Christmas cookie, cut into people, star, moose, heart, and pig shapes, and often hanging from red satin ribbons in windows. During the holidays, I too make dozens of these fragrant cookies to decorate our house. One year, I covered our entire tree with heart-shaped *pepperkaker*. We left for a week between Christmas and New Year, our tree still trimmed. When we returned home, the tree was cookie-less! Lonely ribbon strands hung from the fir boughs. "What in the world," I thought, "did someone come in and eat our cookies?" Apparently so. That someone was a mouse! Despite our thief (or thieves), we still bake these cookies annually, perfuming our house with *pepperkakers'* sweet scent.

MAKES ABOUT 70 COOKIES

3 1/2 cups all-purpose flour
1 teaspoon baking soda
1/2 teaspoon salt
2 teaspoons ground ginger
1 teaspoon ground allspice
1 teaspoon ground cinnamon
1/2 teaspoon ground cloves
1/2 teaspoon ground cardamom
1/4 teaspoon ground black pepper
8 tablespoons (1 stick) unsalted butter, at room temperature
3/4 cup dark molasses
1/2 cup sugar
2 tablespoons heavy cream
White Royal Icing (page 66) for decorating

1. In a bowl, stir together the flour, baking soda, salt, ginger, allspice, cinnamon, cloves, cardamom, and pepper.

2. Put the butter, molasses, and sugar in a pan over medium heat, stirring constantly until the sugar is completely dissolved.

3. Remove from the heat and whisk in the cream until fully incorporated. Stir in the dry ingredients until a dough forms. Form two disks with the dough and wrap with plastic. Chill overnight.

4. After the dough has chilled and you're ready to roll out your cookies, preheat the oven to 350°F and line two baking sheets with parchment paper.

5. Remove one disk of dough from the refrigerator and roll it out 1/8 inch thick on a lightly floured surface. Cut out shapes using cookie cutters. (If you're going to hang the cookies as decorations, use a wooden skewer to make a small hole at the top of each cookie before baking.) Transfer to the prepared baking sheets, placing them 1/2 inch apart.

6. Bake for 10 minutes. Let cool on the baking sheets for 5 minutes before transferring the cookies to a wire rack to cool completely. Repeat the rolling, cutting, baking, and cooling with the second disk of chilled dough.

7. Decorate with royal icing.

CHRISTMAS DAY STEAMED CRANBERRY ROLL

My Grandma has made her cranberry roll for every Christmas dinner I can remember. The moist, steamed dessert is not a roll at all, but a dense molded cake (like a British pudding), laden with tangy cranberries and served with a thick, very sweet hard sauce (my grandmother always left out the brandy, which I now have added back into her recipe, hence the name "hard" sauce). Because my grandmother started making these pudding cakes in multiples at the holidays, she used tin cans instead of pudding molds to steam them, and the shape became cylindrical, so she called them rolls. Not only does this rich dessert satisfy my usually insatiable sweet tooth, it also brings an emotional memory to holidays celebrated and good times shared. There are many advantages to this dessert: It's elegant—a deep-colored fragrant round studded with bright red cranberries—and several may be made at once. The very best thing: It freezes beautifully, and can be made ahead—way ahead. You may also double this recipe, keeping a few cakes tucked in the freezer for unexpected guests.

SERVES 8
CRANBERRY ROLLS
2 cups fresh cranberries, cut in half
$1^1/3$ cups all-purpose flour
2 teaspoons baking soda
$1/3$ cup boiling water
$1/2$ teaspoon salt
1 large egg, lightly beaten
2 tablespoons sugar
$1/2$ cup light molasses
1 teaspoon grated orange zest
1 teaspoon pure vanilla extract

HARD SAUCE
2 cups sugar
8 ounces (2 sticks) unsalted butter
4 tablespoons all-purpose flour
1 teaspoon pure vanilla extract
$1^1/3$ cups half-and-half
Pinch of salt
2 tablespoons brandy

1. Make the cranberry rolls: Grease 3 number-2 size tin cans (a 20-ounce can that holds about $2^1/2$ cups) or a 6-cup steamer mold with baking spray.

2. In a small bowl, toss the cranberries with $1/3$ cup of the flour. In another small bowl, dissolve the baking soda in the boiling water. Stir in the salt.

3. Mix the egg, sugar, and molasses together in a large bowl. Add the baking soda mixture and stir thoroughly. Gently fold in the remaining 1 cup flour. Mix until just blended. Stir in the orange zest and vanilla extract. Fold in the floured cranberries.

4. Fill the cans or steamer mold three-quarters full. Close the steamer mold or, if using cans, cover the tops with aluminum foil securing them with rubber bands.

5. Place the mold or cans in a large stockpot filled with water to just below the tops of the cans (be careful not to get any water in the cans) or mold. Bring the water to a boil, then turn the heat down to keep it at a simmer, cover the stockpot, and steam for 1 hour, 30 minutes. Check the pudding cake with a toothpick, which should come out clean. Let cool for 20 minutes, then unmold.

6. Meanwhile, make the hard sauce: Put all the ingredients in a saucepan. Stirring constantly, cook over medium heat until the sauce has thickened, 3 to 5 minutes.

7. Serve the hard sauce warm over individual slices of cake.

VALENTINE'S DAY CHOCOLATE POPS

Thoughtful gestures are de rigueur at our house on Valentine's Day. There's nothing mandatory about it, no forced extravagant gifts or saccharine store-bought cards. We take it as an opportunity—or excuse— to decorate with hand-cut paper hearts, write kind words, and best of all, hang out and eat chocolate. Making lollipops from melted chocolate is intriguing for kids, and a special way to acknowledge the day—they make great gifts, too. These pops are really simple to make, but there's a catch: You must temper the chocolate, which can be tricky. The tempering process is very scientific: It's about heating and cooling the chocolate to align the cocoa butter molecules. If you don't, the chocolate's surface will be dull instead of smooth and glossy. Using a thermometer to gauge the process helps immensely. I know it all seems very detailed, but truly, with a little practice, you'll find these pops a cinch.

MAKES ABOUT 12 POPS
Lollipop sticks and molds*
One 8-ounce block good-quality
    chocolate (white, milk, or dark)

* Lollipop sticks and molds may be
  purchased from many baking stores,
  and even craft stores. There are
  numerous online retailers, including
  sugarcraft.com.

1. Place the lollipop sticks in the molds.

2. Chop the chocolate into small pieces. Melt half of it in a double boiler over very gently simmering, not boiling, water. Stir constantly while the chocolate melts. Be careful to not let one drop of water touch the chocolate. Using a candy thermometer, check the temperature, which should be between 110 and 115°F. Do not let the chocolate exceed 115°F.

3. Remove the chocolate from the heat, again being careful not to let any moisture into the chocolate. Add the remaining half of the chocolate, a little at a time, into the melted chocolate, stirring vigorously. This will help make the chocolate shine. The goal is to cool the chocolate to 90°F. It may take up to 15 minutes.

4. When the chocolate has cooled to 90°F, test it by spreading a small amount on a piece of wax paper and putting it in the refrigerator. If, after a few minutes, the chocolate is shiny, you're good to go. If it's streaky or dull, you may want to start over with new chocolate. (Perhaps the chocolate was overheated or came in contact with water—you can use it for baking.)

5. There are many ways to fill the molds: (1) Simply use a spoon. (2) Put the tempered chocolate in a sealable plastic baggie, cut off a corner, and squeeze it out into the mold. (3) Place the chocolate in a plastic squeeze bottle and use it to fill the molds (a great option for young children).

6. Tap the mold gently on the counter to remove any air bubbles. Put the molds in the refrigerator to harden for about 10 minutes.

7. Remove from the refrigerator and gently unmold (if the chocolate sticks, freeze for 1 hour, then try to unmold).

JIM'S STAR STRAWBERRY RHUBARB PIE

My husband has been requesting a birthday pie, instead of cake, for years. Not because he's a trendsetter (believe me, he'd be happy to live in the eighteenth century) but because he prefers flavor-rich fruit to sugary-sweet cakes. This strawberry rhubarb pie, decorated with stars, is not innovative or new, but just a good old-fashioned tasty pie.

SERVES 8

3 1/2 cups rhubarb, cut into 1/2-inch pieces

2 cups sliced strawberries

1/4 cup all-purpose flour

1 cup sugar

1 tablespoon lemon juice

1 batch Flaky Pie Crust Dough (page 11)

2 tablespoons unsalted butter, cut into 1/4-inch pieces

1. Preheat the oven to 425°F.

2. In a large bowl, toss together the rhubarb, strawberries, flour, sugar, and lemon juice. Let stand for 15 minutes.

3. Roll out two 11-inch round piecrust circles and, using a cookie cutter, cut a few stars from the extra dough.

4. Line a 9-inch pie plate with one piecrust, leaving a 1-inch overhang.

5. Stir the filling thoroughly and pour it into the pie shell. Dot the filling with the butter pieces. Place the other piecrust gently on top of the filling, sealing the edges by folding the top edge down over the bottom edge and pressing them together. Crimp as desired.

6. Arrange the dough stars decoratively on top of the pie and, using a knife, cut a few vents (slits) in the top crust. Put the pie plate on an aluminum foil–lined baking sheet and bake for 25 minutes, then lower the oven temperature to 350°F and bake for another 25 to 30 minutes, until nicely browned. After 35 minutes of baking time (if not sooner), cover the edges of the pie with a shield or foil to prevent burning.

7. Remove from the oven and let the pie stand for 1 hour before serving.

BOSTON CREAM PIE

Before German Chocolate Cake became my birthday cake of choice, it was Boston Cream Pie. Not a pie at all, this cake does, true to the first word of its name, originate in Boston. Massachusetts's state dessert is still served at the Omni Parker House (formerly the Parker House Hotel), where it was created in the mid-nineteenth century. Silken custard between two sponge cake layers covered with chocolate ganache is a wickedly good combination. My husband, too, when he was young, chose this cake for his birthday celebrations. Perhaps our love was written in the cakes.

SERVES 8 TO 10
SPONGE
3 large eggs, separated, at room
    temperature
1/2 cup granulated sugar
1 teaspoon pure vanilla extract
1 cup cake flour
1 teaspoon baking powder
1/4 teaspoon salt

PASTRY CREAM
4 large egg yolks
1/3 cup sugar
3 tablespoons all-purpose flour
2 cups milk
One 4-inch piece vanilla bean
1/4 teaspoon salt

GANACHE
4 ounces semisweet chocolate, roughly
    chopped
1/4 cup heavy cream
1 tablespoon unsalted butter

1. Make the sponge: Preheat the oven to 350°F. Grease one 9-inch-round cake pan with baking spray.

2. In the bowl of a stand mixer fitted with the whisk attachment, beat the egg whites for 2 minutes, then add 1/4 cup of the sugar. Continue beating until stiff peaks form. Set aside.

3. In a large bowl, beat the egg yolks and the remaining 1/4 cup sugar. Add the vanilla extract and stir. Gently fold in the egg whites. Sprinkle in the flour, baking powder, and salt and continue to fold the batter until all the dry ingredients are incorporated. Pour into the prepared pan and bake for 20 minutes, or until golden and the cake springs back when pressed lightly with your finger. Let cool in the pan for 10 minutes before turning out onto a wire rack to cool completely.

4. Meanwhile, make the pastry cream: Whisk together the egg yolks, sugar, and flour in a heatproof bowl.

5. Put the milk in a saucepan. Split the vanilla bean in half lengthwise and scrape the seeds into the milk and add the pod. Cook over medium-high heat until steaming and bubbling.

6. Slowly pour the heated liquid in a thin stream into the egg mixture while constantly stirring. Pour the mixture back into the saucepan, add the salt, and cook over medium-low heat, stirring constantly, until it thickens and coats the back of a spoon, about 5 minutes. Remove from the heat and let cool.

7. Make the ganache: Put the chocolate and cream in a small saucepan and cook over medium heat, stirring constantly, until melted, about 3 minutes. Remove from the heat and stir in the butter until melted and fully incorporated. Set aside to cool.

8. When the cake is cooled, split it in half horizontally. Place one cake layer on a serving plate and spread the pastry cream evenly over the top. Place the second cake layer on top of the cream. Gently pour the ganache over the cake top. Refrigerate for 2 hours, and up to 24 hours. Let stand for 15 minutes at room temperature before serving.

KIDS' FAVORITE BUNNY CAKE

My father introduced our family to this rich, dense cake that keeps well and stays moist for days. He may not have many recipes in his repertoire but those he does are superb. One Easter my father declared his next culinary undertaking: a bunny cake. Visions of sticky surfaces and burned fingers danced in my head, but I bit my tongue, smiled, and withdrew to the living room. Several hours later my kids came running in, "Come see what we made with Pop Pop. It's awesome." And it was—a big, beautiful, fluffy white bunny.

SERVES 12

CAKE

2 cups cake flour

1/2 teaspoon kosher salt

8 ounces (2 sticks) unsalted butter, at room temperature

2 cups sugar

4 large eggs, at room temperature

2/3 cup canned sweetened cream of coconut, such as Coco Lopez

3 tablespoons milk

1/2 teaspoon pure vanilla extract

1 teaspoon coconut extract

1 cup flaked sweetened coconut

FROSTING

3 large egg whites, at room temperature

3/4 cup sugar

1/4 teaspoon cream of tartar

Pinch of salt

1/3 cup boiling water

2 teaspoons pure vanilla extract

DECORATION

Jellybeans for eyes and nose

Pink vellum paper for ears

One 14-ounce bag flaked sweetened coconut

Green food coloring

1. Make the cake: Preheat the oven to 350°F. Line the bottoms of a 9-inch and 5-inch cake pan with parchment paper and grease.

2. Combine the flour and salt in a bowl.

3. In the bowl of a stand mixer fitted with the paddle attachment, cream the butter and sugar until light and fluffy, about 5 minutes. Add the eggs one at a time, beating well after each addition.

4. Combine the cream of coconut and milk in a small bowl. Alternately add the flour and milk mixtures to the creamed butter mixture, beginning and ending with the flour. Stir in the vanilla and coconut extracts. Fold in the coconut.

5. Divide the batter evenly among the two prepared pans and one standard muffin cup and bake the muffin cup for 20 to 25 minutes and the cake pans for 55 to 65 minutes, or until a toothpick inserted in the center of a cake comes out clean. If the top becomes golden before the baking time ends, cover the pans loosely with aluminum foil. Let cool for 15 minutes in the pans, then turn the cakes out onto wire racks to cool completely.

6. Meanwhile, make the frosting: Put the egg whites, sugar, cream of tartar, and salt in a heatproof bowl of a stand mixer. Add the boiling water and stir until the sugar is dissolved. Beat the mixture on high using the whisk attachment until glossy and peaks form, up to 10 minutes. Gently stir in the vanilla extract.

7. To assemble, cut the 9-inch cake round in half. Place the halves rounded side up on a serving platter, completely aligning them to form the body. Gently push three bamboo skewers through both cake halves to secure them together. Trim off one-quarter of the 5-inch cake round and secure the larger piece as the head of the body with another bamboo skewer. Finally secure the muffin as the tail. Frost the cake and sprinkle with 1 cup of the coconut. Place the rest of the coconut in a small bowl, add a few drops of green food coloring, and toss evenly. Sprinkle the green-colored coconut around the bunny cake. Decorate with jellybeans as eyes and a nose and the vellum paper for the ears.

NOT-SO-GERMAN GERMAN'S CHOCOLATE CAKE

Before my father became deeply obsessed with dark chocolate, German's Chocolate Cake was one of his favorites. He chose it not because of his German heritage—the cake has nothing to do with Germany—but because he loves coconut and pecan, which infuses the caramel frosting that thickly coats this chocolate layer cake. Sam German developed a sweet chocolate for the Baker's Chocolate Company, which was later used in a recipe for German's Chocolate Cake published in a Dallas newspaper. Baker's German's Chocolate is still sold today, and a recipe for the cake is printed inside the box. While the coconut-pecan frosting recipe can't be beat (the one below is a slight adaptation), the cake is mild and sweet. The cake used in this recipe doesn't use German's Chocolate at all, but bittersweet chocolate and coffee for a richer flavor. I hope Mr. German wouldn't mind.

SERVES 14
CAKE LAYERS

4 ounces bittersweet chocolate, roughly chopped

2 cups all-purpose flour

$3/4$ cup unsweetened cocoa powder

1 teaspoon baking soda

$1/2$ teaspoon salt

8 ounces (2 sticks) unsalted butter, at room temperature

2 cups sugar

4 large eggs, at room temperature

1 teaspoon pure vanilla extract

1 cup buttermilk

$1/2$ cup cold brewed coffee

FROSTING

4 large egg yolks

One 12-ounce can evaporated milk

12 tablespoons ($1^1/2$ sticks) unsalted butter

$1^1/2$ cups sugar

2 teaspoons pure vanilla extract

$2^3/4$ cups flaked sweetened coconut

$1^2/3$ cups chopped pecans

1. Make the cake layers: Preheat the oven to 350°F. Grease three 9-inch round cake pans with baking spray.

2. In a small saucepan, melt the chocolate over medium heat, then set aside to cool. In a small bowl, whisk together the flour, cocoa powder, baking soda, and salt.

3. In the bowl of a stand mixer fitted with the paddle attachment, cream the butter and sugar together for 4 minutes on medium until light and fluffy, stopping and scraping down the sides of the bowl as needed. Add the eggs one at a time, mixing well after each addition. Add the vanilla extract and melted chocolate. Mix until fully blended, about 30 seconds.

4. Stir together the buttermilk and coffee in a small bowl. In three portions, add the flour alternating with the milk-coffee mixture, beating for 20 seconds after each addition.

5. Pour the batter into the prepared pans. Bake for 35 to 40 minutes, or until a toothpick inserted into the center comes out clean. Let cool for 10 minutes in the pans, then turn out onto wire racks to cool completely.

6. Meanwhile, make the frosting: Whisk together the egg yolks and evaporated milk in a saucepan. Place over medium heat and add the butter and sugar, stirring constantly until melted and starting to bubble gently, about 5 minutes. Turn the heat to low and continue stirring until the mixture is golden brown and coats the back of a spoon, 5 to 8 minutes (10 to 13 minutes total). Remove from the heat and stir in the vanilla extract. Add the coconut and pecans and stir well. Let stand for 30 minutes.

7. Stack all three cake layers with frosting in between and on top.

SUMMER TRIFLE

Guests were arriving at my friend's house when she turned to me with a look of panic, handed me a pound cake, a quart of cream, and berries, and asked me to make a trifle. I had never made one. Thinking it required layers of custard, preserves, and liquor, in addition to fruit and cream, I was feeling intimidated. "Just layer it all," she said simply. With newfound courage, I sliced the cake, macerated the fruit, and whipped the cream. Layer by layer, I stacked the cake, berries, and cream in a vintage crystal pedestal bowl—and I was finished in less than ten minutes! This recipe is a hybrid of a traditional trifle crossed with the one I made that night. Feel free to replace the berries with other fruit, pound cake with sponge, add custard, substitute your favorite preserves or liquor—or a combination of these.

SERVES 12 TO 14
PERFECT POUND CAKE
8 ounces (2 sticks) unsalted butter,
  at room temperature
1 1/2 cups sugar
1/4 teaspoon salt
3 large eggs
2 cups all-purpose flour
1/3 cup heavy cream
1 teaspoon pure vanilla extract

LAYERS
2 pints red raspberries
1 pint blackberries
1 pint strawberries
1/4 cup granulated sugar
1 tablespoon lemon juice
1/4 cup crème de cassis
1/2 cup water
1/2 cup red raspberry preserves
1 quart heavy cream
1/4 cup confectioners' sugar
1 teaspoon pure vanilla extract

1. Preheat the oven to 325°F. Line a 9 x 5-inch loaf pan with parchment paper with a 1-inch overhang on the two long sides of the pan. Grease the pan and parchment using baking spray.

2. In the bowl of a stand mixer fitted with the paddle attachment, beat the butter, sugar, and salt on medium until light and fluffy, about 4 minutes. Add the eggs one at a time, beating well after each. Add 1 cup of the flour, the cream, and then the remaining 1 cup flour, beating well after each. Stir in the vanilla extract.

3. Pour the batter into the prepared pan and bake for 1 hour, 30 minutes, or until a toothpick inserted in the center comes out with just a few crumbs attached. Let cool on a wire rack for 10 minutes, then turn out onto the rack to cool completely.

4. Meanwhile, set aside a few choice berries for the top of the trifle. Put the rest of the berries in a large bowl and toss with the granulated sugar and lemon juice. Let stand for 20 minutes.

5. Mix the cassis with the water and preserves in a small saucepan and cook over medium heat, stirring constantly, until the mixture comes to a boil. Remove from the heat and set aside.

6. When the pound cake has cooled, cut it into 1-inch slices.

7. In the bowl of a stand mixer fitted with the whisk attachment, whip the cream until thickened, but still soft. Stir in the confectioners' sugar and vanilla extract with a spoon.

8. Line the bottom of a large dish or 3-quart trifle bowl with one third of the slices of pound cake. Do not overlap or layer the cake; trim as necessary to fit. Lightly brush the cake with the cooled preserve mixture. Spoon one third of the berries over the cake layer and top with one third of the whipped cream. Repeat this procedure two more times (there will be three cake layers in all). Decorate the top of the trifle with the reserved berries and chill in the refrigerator for up to 24 hours before serving.

TRIFLE BOWL TIRAMISU

Not for the faint of heart, this recipe requires work. You need to follow countless steps, use many bowls, and buy infrequently used items (espresso powder, mascarpone cheese) to make this layered, light, yet rich Italian dessert. Boy, is it worth the effort, though. One mouthful of creamy sweetness balanced by a smooth, roasted coffee flavor rounded out with a spongy cake for added substance, and you'll immediately understand why. Assembled in a glass trifle bowl, this particular tiramisu, with lush visible layers, makes a stunning presentation. It's big enough to serve to a crowd, is celebration-worthy, and the perfect ending to a lively dinner party.

SERVES 14 TO 16

CAKE LAYERS

2 cups all-purpose flour

2 1/2 teaspoons baking powder

1/2 teaspoon salt

4 large eggs, at room temperature

1 cup sugar

1 cup whole milk

3 tablespoons unsalted butter, at room temperature

1 teaspoon pure vanilla extract

COFFEE SYRUP

1/4 cup sugar

3 tablespoons instant espresso powder

1 cup water

CREAM FILLING

5 large eggs, separated, at room temperature

3/4 cup sugar

1 cup heavy cream

1 pound mascarpone cheese

1/3 cup finely grated bittersweet chocolate

1. Make the cake layers: Preheat the oven to 350°F. Line the bottoms of two 8-inch round cake pans with parchment paper and grease with baking spray.

2. Stir together the flour, baking powder, and salt in a bowl.

3. In the bowl of a stand mixer fitted with the paddle attachment, beat the eggs on high until thick, about 5 minutes. Add the sugar and beat on medium-high for another 3 minutes. Add the flour mixture and mix on low until just incorporated.

4. Put the milk and butter in a small saucepan and heat until the butter is melted and the milk is steaming. Add the hot milk-butter mixture and vanilla extract to the batter and stir until combined.

5. Divide the batter evenly between the prepared pans. Tap each pan on the countertop to eliminate any air bubbles. Bake for 20 to 25 minutes, or until a toothpick inserted in the center of a cake comes out clean. Let cool in the pan for 10 minutes, then turn out onto a wire rack to cool completely.

6. Meanwhile, make the syrup and filling: Bring the sugar, espresso powder, and water to a boil over medium-high heat and continue to simmer until the sugar is dissolved. Set aside to cool.

7. In the bowl of the stand mixer fitted with the whisk attachment, beat the egg whites on medium-high for 2 minutes. Add 1/4 cup of the sugar and continue to beat until firm peaks form. Transfer to another bowl and set aside.

8. Wipe out the mixer bowl, add the cream, and beat until it holds stiff peaks. Transfer to a third bowl.

9. Wipe out the mixer bowl and add the egg yolks and remaining 1/2 cup sugar. Beat for 4 to 5 minutes, until thick and pale yellow in color. Add the cheese and beat until incorporated. Fold the whipped cream into the yolk-cheese mixture until just combined. Gently fold in the egg whites until thoroughly mixed.

10. Split each cooled cake horizontally in half to yield four layers. Place one cake layer in the bottom of a 3-quart trifle bowl (or any 3-quart container). Spread or brush 1/4 cup of the coffee syrup over the cake layer. Next spread one quarter of the cream filling over the coffee-soaked cake. Place another layer of cake over the cream, trimming it to fit if necessary, and spread another ¼ cup coffee syrup and one quarter of cream over the cake.

11. Repeat this two more times with the remaining two cake layers. The layers should just reach the top of the dish, but use your judgment as you're layering and use less filling if needed (or a thin layer could be trimmed off the cake). The final cream layer should just be flush with the top of the dish. Sprinkle the grated chocolate evenly over the top cream layer.

12. Cover and chill for at least 4 hours and up to 1 day before serving.

RED RASPBERRY SORBET

Red raspberries, like sour cherries, tend to make me a little cuckoo. Although raspberries are available year-round in stores, they're very expensive, and not as flavorful as the freshly picked berries we harvest locally. During the summer, my daughters and I frequent Grieg Farm in Red Hook, New York, to pick strawberries, blueberries, and of course—red raspberries. Thorns be damned, I gather those raspberries at any cost (which includes bee stings, pricker scratches, and sunburn), not satisfied until quarts and quarts of the sweet red fruit are collected. Balancing baskets in both arms, I overfill my containers. Inevitably I'll mutter during the car ride home, "What was I thinking?" But then I'll think, "Sorbet, that's what I was thinking!"

MAKES ABOUT 1½ PINTS

1 cup sugar
1/2 cup water
3 cups fresh raspberries
2 teaspoons lemon juice
1/4 cup Chambord or framboise

1. In a small saucepan, heat the sugar and water together over medium-high heat, stirring occasionally, until the sugar dissolves. Set aside to cool.

2. In a blender, puree the raspberries and strain into a bowl, discarding the seeds. Stir in the sugar solution, lemon juice, and Chambord.

3. Refrigerate for at least 3 hours, then freeze in an ice cream maker according to the manufacturer's instructions.

GOLDEN LEMON CURD CAKES

Curd requires patience, something my mother has lots of, which must explain why she doesn't tire when making batch after batch of this delectable fruit spread. Moist and rich, these individual cakes are adapted from my great-grandmother's Gold Cake. The curd adds a creamy center, and a dollop of whipped cream balances the tart lemon flavor. One more little spoonful of curd on top gives an added oomph to these luscious lemon desserts, which make a nice ending to a spring brunch.

MAKES 12 CAKES

CURD FILLING

1 cup sugar

2 tablespoons cornstarch

5 large egg yolks

1/2 cup lemon juice

6 tablespoons unsalted butter, diced

1 tablespoon grated lemon zest

CAKES

2 cups all-purpose flour

1 tablespoon baking powder

1/2 teaspoon salt

8 tablespoons (1 stick) unsalted butter, at room temperature

1 cup sugar

1/3 cup egg yolks (about 6 large yolks)

1/2 cup milk

1 teaspoon pure vanilla extract

1 tablespoon grated lemon zest

Whipped cream

1. Make the curd filling: In a double boiler or a metal bowl placed over a pan of simmering water, whisk together the sugar, cornstarch, and egg yolks. Slowly stir in the lemon juice. Stirring constantly, cook over the simmering water for 10 to 12 minutes or until thickened. The curd should coat the back of a wooden spoon.

2. Remove the thickened curd from the heat and let cool for 3 minutes. Stir in the butter and lemon zest. Set aside to cool completely.

3. Make the cakes: Preheat the oven to 350°F. Generously grease a standard 12-cup muffin pan with baking spray.

4. Stir together the flour, baking powder, and salt in a small bowl.

5. In the bowl of a stand mixer fitted with the paddle attachment, cream the butter and sugar until light and fluffy, about 3 minutes, stopping and scraping down the sides of the bowl as necessary. Add the egg yolks and beat on medium for 30 seconds.

6. In three portions, alternately add the flour mixture and the milk to the mixer bowl, beginning and ending with the flour and beating for 15 seconds between additions. Add the vanilla extract and lemon zest and mix until well blended.

7. Pour into the prepared muffin pan and bake for 15 to 18 minutes, or until a toothpick inserted into the center of a cupcake comes out clean. Let cool in the pan for 5 minutes, then gently release the cupcakes onto a wire rack to cool completely.

8. When completely cool, invert the cupcakes so the large side is facing down. Using a teaspoon, remove a scoopful of cake from the center of each inverted cupcake.

9. Fill the center of each cupcake with a spoonful of curd, replace the scooped-out cake, and top with whipped cream and another small spoonful of curd.

HEAVENLY ANGEL FOOD CAKE

This ethereally light, almost weightless cake is a favorite among many of my family members. It has always been my mother's birthday cake of choice, as well as my brother-in-law's. Both prefer it served with fresh berries and whipped cream. When my sister and I were kids, we always made this cake for my mother from a box. It required no eggs, no oil, just water. It couldn't have been easier. These days my daughter Camilla is always begging me to buy the box mix, which I refuse to purchase, as I am turned off by the chemical aftertaste of cakes made from mixes. I suggested we try making a homemade one. Thumbing through my great-grandmother's journal I found this recipe—nothing more than a list of ingredients and a notation of a one-hour bake time (which proved too long for my oven). Although the prep for this recipe is more time-consuming than a box mix requires, even my daughter agrees that the taste is heavenly.

SERVES 10

1 cup cake flour
1 1/2 cups confectioners' sugar
1 1/2 cups egg whites (about 12 large whites), at room temperature
1 1/2 teaspoons cream of tartar
1/4 teaspoon salt
1/2 cup granulated sugar
1 teaspoon pure vanilla extract
Fresh berries
Whipped cream

1. Preheat the oven to 350°F.

2. Sift together the flour and confectioners' sugar into a small bowl.

3. Put the egg whites in the bowl of a stand mixer fitted with the whisk attachment. Beat on high for 1 minute, or until slightly foamy. Add the cream of tartar and salt. Continue beating on high until soft peaks form. Add the granulated sugar and beat another 30 seconds, or until stiff peaks form. Using a rubber spatula, very gently fold in the flour–confectioners' sugar mixture, 1 cup at a time. Add the vanilla extract and continue to fold the batter, ensuring that all the dry ingredients are fully incorporated.

4. Spoon the batter into an ungreased 10-inch tube pan and bake for 40 minutes.

5. Remove from the oven and invert the pan upside down onto a bottle to cool, about 1 hour. When completely cool, loosen the sides of the cake from the pan with a knife and unmold. Serve with berries and whipped cream.

STRAWBERRY SURPRISE CUPCAKES

Tantalizing with thick frosting and a thin slice of strawberry, these cupcakes are especially hard to resist. The sweet pink color invites you to take a bite, and then the surprise: There's a smidge of strawberry frosting inside the cupcake too. Children and adults alike appreciate the fresh berry flavor—no red food coloring used—paired with the delicate, tender cake. Look for colorful red or pink cupcake liners when baking these adorable cakes.

MAKES 24 CUPCAKES

CUPCAKES

About $3/4$ cup hulled strawberries

$2^1/2$ cups cake flour

$3^1/2$ teaspoons baking powder

8 tablespoons (1 stick) unsalted butter,
   at room temperature

$1^1/4$ cups sugar

2 large egg whites

1 teaspoon pure vanilla extract

1 cup whole milk

STRAWBERRY FROSTING

About $3/4$ cup hulled strawberries, plus
   24 strawberry slices for garnish

12 ounces (3 sticks) unsalted butter,
   at room temperature

$4^1/2$ cups confectioners' sugar

$1^1/2$ teaspoons pure vanilla extract

1. Make the cupcakes: Preheat the oven to 350°F. Line a standard 12-cup muffin pan with paper liners.

2. Puree the strawberries in a food processor or blender. You should get about $1/2$ cup puree; if not, puree a few more strawberries to yield $1/2$ cup. Set aside.

3. In a bowl, sift together the flour and baking powder. Set aside.

4. In the bowl of a stand mixer fitted with the paddle attachment, cream the butter and sugar together on medium-high for 4 minutes. Add the egg whites and beat for 1 minute on medium, stopping and scraping down the sides of the bowl as necessary. Add the strawberry puree and vanilla extract and mix on medium for 30 more seconds.

5. In five portions, alternately add the flour mixture and milk to the mixer bowl, beginning and ending with the flour and mixing well after each addition, about 20 to 30 seconds. Fill the liners halfway with batter and bake for 20 minutes, or until a toothpick inserted in the center of a cupcake comes out clean. Let cool in the pan for 5 minutes, then gently release the cupcakes onto a wire rack to cool completely.

6. Make the strawberry frosting: Puree the strawberries to yield $1/2$ cup. In the bowl of a stand mixer fitted with the paddle attachment, cream the butter for 4 minutes, or until light and fluffy. Add the strawberries and mix. (The mixture may seem curdled, but will come together with the addition of the sugar.) Sift the confectioners' sugar into the bowl 1 cup at a time, mixing well after each addition. Stir in the vanilla extract. Set aside.

7. Using a teaspoon, gently scoop out a spoonful of cake from the center of each cupcake. Fill the cavity with frosting using a pastry bag or plastic bag with the corner snipped off. Replace the scooped-out cake piece. Frost the top of each cupcake and top with a strawberry slice.

BLACK-BOTTOM ICE CREAM PIE ⧗

A dark, heavy chocolate cake has little appeal on a hot, humid August day. Perhaps that's why my sister, Lisa, who favors chocolate over most things, opts for ice cream pie instead of cake for her summer birthday celebration. Unlike a bowl of ice cream, which can't hold many candles, the expanse of this pie gives ample opportunity for ceremonious lighting. True to its name, Black-Bottom Pie has a tasty, dark-colored chocolate crust. A satisfyingly thick, fudgy sauce covers the crust before the ice cream is generously added. Mint chocolate chip is Lisa's preferred flavor, but almost any ice cream will work with this recipe: coffee, strawberry, dulce de leche, or even plain vanilla. Summer birthdays scream for ice cream, but so does any sticky, sweltering day.

SERVES 8

CRUST

1 1/4 cups finely crushed chocolate
　　cookie crumbs (about 25 cookies,
　　such as Famous Chocolate Wafers)
4 tablespoons unsalted butter, melted
2 tablespoons sugar

FILLING

2 ounces unsweetened chocolate
6 tablespoons water
1/2 cup sugar
3 tablespoons unsalted butter
1/4 teaspoon salt
1/2 teaspoon pure vanilla extract
1 quart mint chocolate-chip ice cream
　　(or your favorite flavor)
1/4 cup chocolate cookie crumbs
　　(about 5 wafer cookies)

1. Make the crust: Preheat the oven to 375°F.

2. Put the cookie crumbs, melted butter, and sugar in a bowl and stir to combine.

3. Press the mixture firmly into a 9-inch pie plate, being sure to cover the sides of plate too. Bake for 5 minutes. Remove from the oven and let cool completely.

4. Meanwhile, make the filling: In a small saucepan over medium-low heat, combine the chocolate, water, sugar, butter, and salt. Cook, stirring constantly, until the chocolate has melted. Continue to cook for another 1 minute, or until the mixture has thickened slightly. Do not allow it to boil. Remove from the heat and stir in the vanilla extract.

5. Pour the sauce over the cooled pie crust and place it in the refrigerator to chill for at least 1 hour.

6. Once the sauce has firmed in the crust, soften the ice cream slightly so it will be easy to scoop and spread evenly into the pie crust. Fill the crust with the softened ice cream. Sprinkle the top with the cookie crumbs and freeze the pie for at least 2 hours, or until firm.

WACKY CAKES-IN-A-CONE

One of my proudest first-grade moments, alongside playing Mrs. Rabbit in the school play, was when my mother made cake cones for the class. I beamed as she walked through the door carrying a tray of ice cream cones, topped with thickly swirled chocolate frosting and alit with candles. There was no convincing me otherwise, I truly thought those cones were the coolest birthday treat ever! The Wacky Cake that fills these cones evolved from a tradition that hearkens back to the Depression era, if not earlier, when supplies were short—this cake is eggless and dairy free—and innovation necessary. The wacky reaction of the baking soda and vinegar causes the cake to rise. Part of the wackiness, too, was that the batter was mixed in the pan. Although the batter for these treats is whipped up in one bowl instead, baking it in cones makes it wackier still. With little effort, you too can make a child's heart sing.

MAKES 36 CAKE CONES

WACKY CAKES

3 cups all-purpose flour

2 cups sugar

1/2 cup unsweetened cocoa powder

2 teaspoons baking powder

1 teaspoon salt

2 cups water

3/4 cup canola or vegetable oil

2 tablespoons white vinegar

1 tablespoon pure vanilla extract

36 flat-bottomed ice cream cones

VANILLA FROSTING

8 tablespoons (1 stick) unsalted butter, at room temperature

3 3/4 cups confectioners' sugar

1/4 cup heavy cream, or more as needed

1 teaspoon pure vanilla extract

Multicolored sprinkles

1. Make the wacky cakes: Preheat the oven to 350°F. Place 1 cone in each cup of a standard 12-cup muffin pan (it helps them remain upright when you put them in the oven).

2. Stir the flour, sugar, cocoa powder, baking powder, and salt together in a large mixing bowl. Add the water, oil, vinegar, and vanilla extract and stir until thoroughly combined, at least 150 strokes.

3. Using a 1/4 cup measure, fill each cone about three-quarters full. Bake for 30 minutes, or until a toothpick inserted all the way into a cone comes out clean. Unless you have 2 standard 12-cup muffin pans, you'll need to repeat this twice with the remaining batter. Let cool completely.

4. Meanwhile, make the Vanilla Frosting: In the bowl of a stand mixer fitted with the whisk attachment, beat the butter for 4 minutes, or until light and fluffy. Slowly add half of the confectioners' sugar until fully incorporated. Add the cream and continue to beat until smooth and creamy. Continue to add the remaining sugar and beat until your desired consistency is reached, adding more sugar or cream as necessary. Beat in the vanilla extract.

5. Frost the wacky cake cones and decorate with sprinkles.

NOTE: An empty egg carton makes a great container for holding and transporting the cones.

GIVING

It is possible to give without loving,
but it is impossible to love without giving.

—UNKNOWN

When I receive a handmade gift, I feel loved. There is no other way to describe the warmth I feel when someone has taken the time to make something— just for me. Whether it's a card my daughter has artistically crafted or a scarf my aunt has knit, the time and thought is worth more than any store-bought good. Opening a box from Tiffany's is exciting, but there are hundreds more of that same necklace out there. A homemade gift is an original.

One of the best gifts I ever received arrived a week or so after my second daughter, Camilla, was born. We had just driven up to our country house, there was no food in the fridge, I had a newborn stuck to my breast, a toddler running around, and my husband, Jim, was exhausted. We couldn't even imagine driving to town, only ten minutes away, to get dinner. As if a little angel descended upon our house, my neighbor Robin appeared with no warning, holding forth a beautiful antique platter replete with a whole roasted duck, salad picked from her garden, and perfectly browned potatoes. She said she knew we must be tired, and wanted us to enjoy the meal at our leisure. We didn't wait another minute; as soon as she left we dove right in. Suddenly there was another knock at the door, and a second neighbor, MJ, presented a peach pie. The two women hadn't discussed their offerings, but what a perfect present. My husband and I were elated, our bellies—and hearts—were full.

My grandmother is one of those women who is always baking for someone or something. Whether she's mixing up a batch of cookies or bars for a ladies' group or making coffeecakes by the dozen for a church function, she is rarely without a container full of sweets ready to give. Another close family friend, Jeanne, has inspired me greatly in the gift-giving arena. Every Christmas my family receives a tin filled with sweets from her—*pepperkaker* or homemade walnut candies. One of the most giving people I know, Jeanne bakes for her thirty-something son's office weekly. She was going to Hawaii for an extended trip and Aaron's colleagues weren't sure what they'd do without her goodies. Jeanne made six weeks' worth of treats and froze them, ready for her son to bring in her absence, maintaining the five-year tradition.

Baking is an artistic expression, and doing it for others demonstrates thought, an investment of time, and care. Recipients feel loved, and the gift-giver feels a sense of gratification. Using a favorite family recipe when making gifts is doubly special. You're sharing a treasured tradition, and a sweet to eat. Who can deny the goodness of that?

PERSONALIZING AND PACKAGING BAKED GOODS

1. ALWAYS ATTACH A RECIPE CARD There are many online options for purchasing and downloading recipe card templates, which you may then personalize with your own recipes. Check out lovevsdesign.com and skiptomylou.org for free online printable downloads.

2. USE INTERESTING CONTAINERS Consider reusing jelly jars, coffee tins, oatmeal canisters, and wooden fruit crates. Wrapping paper or spray paint will give these items a new look. Containerstore.com sells a wide array of boxes and tins, such as Chinese take-out cartons and paint-can canisters.

3. BE CREATIVE WITH YOUR WRAPPING Use cellophane wrap, glassine bags, and colored wax paper squares. Fancyflours.com has a large selection of packaging supplies. Wrap items like tea towels around wooden boxes and cloth napkins around bundles of cookies.

4. GIVE YOUR GIFT IN A PUDDING MOLD OR BUNDT PAN Instead of giving a steamed pudding mold or bundt pan empty, give it full! Bake a cake or pudding right in the pan. Be sure to include a recipe so the recipient can use it again.

5. ATTACH VINTAGE COOKIE CUTTERS Thrift stores and tag sales are prime places to find antique cookie cutters. Purchase them in summer to give in the winter. Attach with ribbon and recipe to your favorite cut-out cookies. Sugarcraft.com offers a large selection of new cookie cutters.

6. PACKAGE YOUR DESSERT WITH A SPECIAL INGREDIENT If nutmeg or vanilla bean is a key ingredient to your recipe, include a small jar or package of it with the dessert you're giving.

7. PERSONALIZE A TRAY Découpage recipes and photos on the bottom of a wooden tray or glass plate. Package your treats on it, and when the recipient finishes the goodies, he'll find a sweet surprise! Behrenbergglass.com sells a variety of glass plates, and the site gives detailed découpage instructions too.

8. BAKE IN DIPSOSABLE PAPER PANS Italian-made paper pans are my favorite way to package breads and cakes (no pans to wash on your end). They are extremely difficult to find in stores, though. I make it easy and place a big order to keep a supply on hand. Bakedeco.com sells a variety of shapes and sizes.

9. ATTACH A RECIPE MAGNET TO A TIN Give your goods in a food-grade tin container and design a recipe magnet to decorate the lid. Both the tin and magnet are functional after they serve their original purpose. Papermart.com offers many types of tins.

10. RECIPE CARD CLOTHESLINE Tie your wrapped gift with a ribbon clothesline and affix several of your favorite recipes with colored clothespins. The clothesline, hung across a shelf or wall, doubles as a functional recipe display and kitchen decoration.

PUMPKIN SNACK BREAD

There's nothing like the bittersweet smell of fall signaling long summer days behind you and cold winter nights ahead. The scent of the crisp air is tinged with burning fires and falling leaves. Baking this fragrant bread, with its notes of ginger, cloves, and allspice, will fill your house with the smell of autumn. A thick slice of this moist loaf is the perfect after-school snack. It also packs well in lunches. I prefer to use corn oil in this recipe, but any vegetable oil will do. Because it's even better eaten the next day, this bread, like most quick breads, is excellent for gift giving. I like to bake it in mini-loaf Italian paper molds, available from bakedeco.com, so I can give it to several people at once—teachers, colleagues, neighbors. Doubling the recipe will yield ten mini loaves.

MAKES ONE 8¹/₂ X 4¹/₂ X 2³/₄-INCH LOAF OR FIVE 4 X 2 X 2-INCH MINI LOAVES

1³/₄ cups all-purpose flour

³/₄ cups granulated sugar

¹/₂ cup firmly packed light brown sugar

1 teaspoon baking soda

¹/₂ teaspoon salt

1 teaspoon ground cinnamon

¹/₂ teaspoon ground ginger

¹/₄ teaspoon ground cloves

¹/₄ teaspoon ground allspice

1 cup canned pumpkin puree

¹/₂ cup corn oil

¹/₃ cup orange juice

2 large eggs, at room temperature

1. Preheat the oven to 350°F. Line a loaf pan with parchment paper, leaving one extra inch of paper extending beyond the two long sides of the pan. Grease the pan and paper with baking spray. If using paper pans, skip the parchment but still grease with baking spray.

2. Stir together the flour, sugars, baking soda, salt, and spices in a large bowl until thoroughly combined.

3. In another bowl, whisk together the pumpkin, oil, orange juice, and eggs. Add the wet ingredients to the dry, stirring with a wooden spoon until well combined. Do not overmix.

4. Pour the batter into the prepared pan and bake for 1 hour and 15 minutes (35 to 40 minutes for mini loaves), or until a toothpick inserted into the center of the loaf comes out clean.

5. Let the bread cool for 10 minutes in the pan, then gently lift the loaf out and place it on a rack to cool completely for 1 hour. If baking in paper pans, do not remove from the pans until eaten. The bread is even better the next day, so if you can resist, wrap with aluminum foil and leave at room temperature overnight.

MELISSA'S MAPLE LEAF COOKIES

Many of my favorite cookie recipes come from holiday cookie swaps, including this charming maple leaf confection from Melissa Thongs. She brought a large tray of these thin, buttery cookies with a hint of maple to a swap and I've been hooked ever since. I've heightened the maple flavor with a creamy icing that also has traces of the syrup's earthy sweet flavor. Melissa, whose son lives in Vermont, often gives small, leaf-shaped containers of this liquid gold at holidays. A package of maple sugar (available from kingarthurflour.com or in health food stores), a bottle of maple syrup, a cookie cutter (sets of 5 from sugarcraft.com), and the recipe make a perfect accompaniment to a tin of these divine cookies.

MAKES ABOUT 2 DOZEN MAPLE COOKIES

2 cups all-purpose flour

1/2 cup maple sugar

1/4 teaspoon salt

8 tablespoons (1 stick) unsalted butter, at room temperature

1/4 cup maple syrup

MAPLE ICING

3/4 cup confectioners' sugar

3 tablespoons maple syrup

1 tablespoon heavy cream

1/8 teaspoon natural maple flavoring

1. Make the maple cookies: Sift together the flour, maple sugar, and salt. (Be sure to completely break up any sugar clumps.)

2. In the bowl of a stand mixer fitted with the paddle attachment, cream the butter for 3 minutes. Add the maple syrup and mix to combine. Blend on medium-high for 1 minute.

3. With the mixer on low, gradually add the flour mixture and continue beating until fully incorporated. Shape the dough into a disk, cover with plastic wrap, and chill for 1 hour.

4. When you're ready to roll out the cookies, preheat the oven to 350°F. Line two baking sheets with parchment paper.

5. Place the dough on a lightly floured surface and roll out to 1/8 inch thick. Cut using maple leaf cutters and transfer with a spatula to the prepared baking sheets. Place in the freezer for 30 minutes.

6. Bake for 15 to 17 minutes, or until lightly golden. Transfer the cookies to wire racks set over wax paper.

7. Make the maple icing: Whisk all the ingredients together in a bowl until smooth. Pour over the cookies. After about 10 minutes, use a skewer to create veins in the leaves.

LA & JUDITH'S DRIED CHERRY OATMEAL COOKIES

I know a mother-daughter team who can cook like no other. When you attend a dinner, party, or even a picnic-to-go they've prepared, you know you're in for a treat. Wherever they go, those two always bring food with them to share. Judith Bromley and La Scanlon pull out all the stops when they cook, using only the very best ingredients, many procured from the upstate New York farmers' markets where La often works. This cookie recipe, inspired by La and Judith, is packed with lots of delicious morsels. When I first tasted Judith's oatmeal cookies, it had dried cherries and white chocolate chips. La loaded hers with nuts, semisweet chocolate, and coconut, too. You can easily modify this cookie with your favorite choice tidbits—nuts, chips, or dried fruit. Just keep your add-in amounts to less than 4 cups.

MAKES 4 TO 5 DOZEN COOKIES

1^3/4 cups spelt flour

1 teaspoon baking soda

^{1}/2 teaspoon salt

8 ounces (2 sticks) unsalted butter, at room temperature

1^1/4 cups firmly packed brown sugar

^{1}/2 cup sugar

2 large eggs, at room temperature

2 teaspoons pure vanilla extract

3 cups old-fashioned rolled oats

1 cup pecans, chopped

1 cup sweetened flaked coconut

1 cup dried cherries

1. Preheat the oven to 350°F. Line two baking sheets with parchment paper.

2. Stir the flour, baking soda, and salt together in a small bowl. Set aside.

3. In the bowl of a stand mixer fitted with the paddle attachment, cream the butter and sugars on medium-high for 2 minutes, stopping and scraping down the sides of the bowl with a rubber spatula as necessary.

4. Add the eggs one at a time, beating thoroughly after each addition. Stir in the vanilla extract. Add the dry ingredients and mix on low until just incorporated. Do not overbeat.

5. Using a wooden spoon, stir in the oats, then the pecans, coconut, cherries, or other add-ins. Your total amount of chips, nuts, fruit, and/or coconut should not exceed 4 cups.

6. Using a 1^1/2-tablespoon ice cream scoop, form round balls and place 2 inches apart on the prepared baking sheets. Lightly flatten each dough ball with your fingers.

7. Bake for 6 to 9 minutes. The cookies will not look done but remove them from the oven after 9 minutes to prevent over-baking—the cookies will become hard quickly. Let the cookies cool for 5 minutes on the baking sheet before transferring them to a wire rack to cool completely.

Left: La & Judith's Dried Cherry Oatmeal Cookies
Middle: Worth-the-Wait Chocolate Chip Cookies
Right: Melissa's Maple Leaf Cookies

WORTH-THE-WAIT CHOCOLATE CHIP COOKIES

The ubiquitous chocolate chip cookie—it's almost as American as apple pie. But oh, how the cookies can differ. Some are small, thick, and crunchy, others soft and large. My mother always uses the Toll House cookie recipe straight from the back of the bright yellow chip package. Her dough results in cookies with thin edges surrounding a soft, bulging middle section. The cookies have no crisp and they are soft and sweet. They are the cookies I knew and loved as a child.

My older sister's chocolate chip cookies are different from Mom's—they have the slightest bit of crisp surrounding a soft, chewy sumptuous center. Oh my, they are good! Her secret? More flour and vanilla.

A few years ago in a *New York Times* article, David Leite sought out the perfect chocolate chip cookie, with one significant conclusion among several: Chilling the dough deepens the flavor.

This recipe incorporates all those finds. The dough yields a slightly crisp cookie with a chewy, moist center possessing a deep flavor rich with caramel and butter notes. The 24- to 36-hour wait time for the dough to chill may be a deterrent for some, but those who persist will find it's worth it.

MAKES 3¹/₂ DOZEN COOKIES

3 cups all-purpose flour
1 teaspoon baking soda
1 teaspoon baking powder
¹/₂ teaspoon salt
8 ounces (2 sticks) unsalted butter,
　at room temperature
1³/₄ cups firmly packed dark brown sugar
¹/₄ cup granulated sugar
1 large egg plus 1 yolk, at room
　temperature
1 tablespoon pure vanilla extract
One 11.5-ounce package Ghiradelli
　60% cacao bittersweet chocolate chips
　(about 1¹/₂ cups)
1 cup chopped pecans (optional)

1. Stir together the flour, baking soda, baking powder, and salt in a bowl.

2. In the bowl of a stand mixer fitted with the paddle attachment, cream the butter and sugars on medium-high for about 3 minutes. Add the egg and yolk and beat on medium until incorporated, stopping and scraping down the sides of the bowl with a rubber spatula as needed. Stir in the vanilla extract. Add the dry ingredients and beat on low until just combined. Stir in the chocolate chips and pecans, if using.

3. Using a 1¹/₂-tablespoon ice cream scoop, form round balls and place them in a sealable container. Refrigerate for 24 to 36 hours.

4. Preheat the oven to 375°F. Line two baking sheets with parchment paper.

5. Remove the dough balls from the refrigerator and place them 2 inches apart on the prepared cookie sheets. Bake for 11 minutes, or until the cookies become ever-so-slightly browned. The cookies may look underbaked when you remove them from the oven but will firm up when cooling (this gives them their chewy texture). You may want to experiment with one or two cookies to determine baking time before baking an entire sheet of them.

6. Allow the cookies to cool on the baking sheet for 5 minutes before transferring them to a wire rack to cool (or eating them warm!).

DREAM BARS

When I was little, my grandmother always arrived at special occasions with several Tupperware containers and sometimes a decorative tin with wax paper peeking out. When I saw that tin I was gleeful because I knew Grandma had made her special Dream Bars. Grandma's original recipe for these chocolatey, nutty coconut bars—known by some as Magic Bars or Seven-Layer bars—called for butterscotch chips, which she always omitted, doubling the chocolate chips instead. I've gone one step further and replaced the sweetened coconut with unsweetened flakes, which makes for a less cloyingly sweet bar, and added nuts to the crust for more texture. The best thing about these bars is that they last. They are so rich and sweet that a small piece is satisfying. You can keep them stored in an airtight container for up to one week, which makes them perfect for gift giving. This recipe makes an extra-large batch so you'll have enough for giving and sending—and some for yourself.

MAKES ABOUT FIFTY 4-INCH TRIANGLES

1 cup walnuts, plus 1 1/4 cups chopped

3 cups finely ground graham crackers (about 20 crackers)

12 tablespoons (1 1/2 sticks) unsalted butter, melted

Two 14-ounce cans sweetened condensed milk

2 cups bittersweet chocolate chips, such as Ghirardelli 60% cacao

2 cups unsweetened flaked coconut*

* If you are unable to find unsweetened flakes, usually found in bulk at health food stores or ethnic sections of the grocery store, shredded coconut may be used.

1. Preheat the oven to 350°F. Line an 11 x 17-inch rimmed baking sheet with parchment paper, leaving a 1-inch overhang on the long sides. Spray the parchment with baking spray.

2. Spread 1 cup walnuts in a single layer on an ungreased baking sheet and bake for 8 to 10 minutes, or until they just start to slightly brown. Keep an eye on them because nuts can burn in the blink of an eye. Check on them several times during baking, stirring if necessary.

3. Place the cooled, toasted walnuts in the bowl of a food processor and run until the nuts are finely ground. Transfer to a bowl. Add the graham cracker crumbs and stir well. Pour in the butter and continue to stir until the mixture is thoroughly moistened.

4. Press the mixture into the prepared baking sheet. Try to eliminate any cracks and make sure the crust is firmly packed using the back of an offset spatula.

5. Pour the sweetened condensed milk evenly over the entire crust. Spread a layer of chocolate chips over the condensed milk. Spread the nuts on top of the chips. Last, sprinkle the coconut on the top.

6. Using an offset spatula, gently press the toppings down into the condensed milk, being careful not to break the crust.

7. Bake for 25 minutes, or until the coconut becomes lightly browned. Remove from the oven and let cool completely. Cut into twenty-five 3 1/2 x 2 1/2-inch squares, then cut those squares in half to make triangles.

BILLIONAIRE BARS

Our family became obsessed with all things Scottish the year my daughter was in sixth grade, under the tutelage of Shirley, a bona fide Scot. She once described, in her lilting and lyrical voice, a special sweet from her childhood, Millionaire Bars: "We would get them from Thornton's, a local candy shop. Little squares of bliss…made with chocolate, caramel, and shortbread, they were so decadent." I was intrigued to try it myself. This recipe starts with my mother-in-law's legendary shortbread recipe for a base, then takes a shortcut using store-bought caramels, and finishes with a creamy layer of milk chocolate. There's a secret, though—use a good-quality caramel, such as Werther's, and the chocolate must be milky, preferably Cadbury's Dairy Milk—and with these decadent ingredients, Scottish Millionaire Bars become Billionaire Bars. After all, isn't today's billionaire yesterday's millionaire?

MAKES 32 BARS

SHORTBREAD

1 cup all-purpose flour

1/4 cup sugar

1 tablespoon cornstarch

Pinch of salt

6 tablespoons cold unsalted butter, cut into 1-inch pieces

CARAMEL TOPPING

11 ounces Werther's Original Chewy Caramels

2 tablespoons heavy cream

CHOCOLATE GLAZE

4 ounces Cadbury's Dairy Milk chocolate

4 tablespoons unsalted butter

1 1/2 teaspoons corn syrup

Top: Billionaire Bars
Bottom: Raspberry Jam Bars

1. Make the shortbread: Grease an 8-inch square tart pan with a removable bottom with baking spray (or line an 8-inch square pan with parchment paper, leaving a 2-inch overhang on two sides, and spray).

2. In the bowl of a food processor, combine the flour, sugar, cornstarch, and salt. Add the butter and process until the dough comes together, about 3 minutes.

3. Press the dough firmly and evenly into the prepared pan. Using a fork, make prick marks all over the dough in a uniform pattern. Place the pan in the refrigerator to chill for 30 minutes.

4. Preheat the oven to 350°F. Bake the chilled dough for 30 to 35 minutes, or until light golden brown. Remove from the oven and let cool completely in the pan.

5. Make the caramel topping: Unwrap the caramels and place in a microwave-safe bowl. Add the cream. Microwave for 2 to 2 1/2 minutes, or until mostly melted. Remove from the microwave and stir rapidly to ensure that all the caramel melts and the cream is fully incorporated. Spread the caramel mixture evenly over the cooled shortbread and let the caramel firm up, about 30 minutes (or you can place in the refrigerator for 15 minutes).

6. Meanwhile, make the glaze: Place the chocolate in a small saucepan. Add the butter and cook over low heat until both are completely melted. Remove from the heat and add the corn syrup. Stir vigorously until fully incorporated. Pour the chocolate mixture on top of the firm caramel, spreading until smooth. Let stand until the chocolate becomes firm, about 1 hour at room temperature.

7. Remove the bars from the pan and cut into 1 x 2-inch diamonds. (If using a pan with parchment, loosen the shortbread on all sides with a sharp knife and carefully lift out of the pan using the parchment overhang as handles.)

RASPBERRY JAM BARS

Birthdays, class celebrations, parties—you name it and Camilla wants to take jam bars. There was one problem, though: the bars I used to make had nuts. With so many allergies and the school's no nut policy, my former bars were not an option. With some revisions, I now make the bars, rich with oats and brown sugar, nut free. If you need a gluten-free option, replace the flour with Bob's Red Mill Gluten-Free All-Purpose Baking Flour. For a thoughtful gift, pair these extremely portable bars with a découpage tray or box. The bar-tray combo makes a great kid's gift too.

MAKES 20 BARS

8 tablespoons (1 stick) unsalted butter
1 cup firmly packed light brown sugar
2 large egg yolks
1^1/2 cups all-purpose flour
1^1/2 cup rolled oats
1 teaspoon baking powder
^{1}/4 teaspoon salt
1^1/4 cups raspberry jam

1. Preheat the oven to 350°F. Line a 9 x 13-inch baking pan with parchment paper, leaving a 1-inch overhang on two opposing sides. Grease the parchment paper and pan with baking spray.

2. In the bowl of a stand mixer fitted with the paddle attachment, cream the butter and brown sugar for 4 minutes on medium-high until light and fluffy, stopping and scraping down the sides as necessary.

3. Add the egg yolks and blend until fully incorporated. Add the flour, oats, baking powder, and salt and mix until thoroughly combined. The mixture will be very crumbly at this point.

4. Scoop out 1 cup of the dough and set aside. Spread the rest of the crumb mixture in the prepared pan. Using your fingers or an offset spatula, press the dough evenly in the pan. Spread the jam carefully over the dough, being careful not to disturb the crust.

5. Sprinkle the remaining dough on top of the jam. Use your fingers to press together a few larger clumps, too. (The majority of the topping should be sprinkled to ensure the entire surface is covered, with a few clumps dotting it here and there.)

6. Bake for 25 minutes. Increase the oven temperature to 375°F and bake for another 5 minutes, or until the topping is the slightest golden brown. Remove from the oven and cool in the pan. Cut into 2^1/2-inch squares and serve.

RENEE'S BEST SHORTBREAD EVER

My mother-in-law, Renee, an energetic, red-haired Scots-Irish woman, made a rich, scrumptious shortbread in the Scottish tradition—buttery, crumbly, and not too sweet. She made batch after batch at the holidays, packaging rounds cut into triangular wedges known as petticoat tails into green and red tins, and gifting them to friends and family. If you weren't lucky enough to be a recipient, you could line up at the church's Fall Fair Plaid Pantry to purchase one of Renee's shortbread rounds for $9— the dozens she donated always sold out quickly. While legend credits Mary, Queen of Scots with the popularity of petticoat tails, Renee and her shortbread have achieved legendary status in our family.

MAKES 16 PETTICOAT TAILS

2 cups all-purpose flour

6 tablespoons sugar

2 tablespoons cornstarch

1/8 teaspoon salt

12 tablespoons (1 1/2 sticks) cold unsalted butter, cut into 1-inch pieces

1. Butter an 8-inch round cake pan.

2. In the bowl of a food processor, combine the flour, sugar, cornstarch, and salt by pulsing 6 to 8 times. Add the butter and process until the dough comes together, 2 to 3 minutes. If the dough only loosely starts to stick together, just gather the dough into a ball with your hands and place it in the prepared pan. The dough should not be crumbly.

3. Press the dough firmly and evenly into the prepared pan. (This step is important to ensure an even texture). Using a fork, make prick marks all over the dough in a uniform pattern. Place the pan in the refrigerator to chill for 30 minutes.

4. Preheat the oven to 350°F.

5. Bake for 30 to 35 minutes, or until pale golden brown. Immediately after you remove the shortbread from the oven, and it's still warm, cut it into 16 petticoat tails (with a sharp knife, cut the round into four quarters, then divide each quarter into four more triangles). Let cool for at least 30 minutes before removing from the pan. Store in an airtight container.

BETTINA'S CHOCOLATE SPICE COOKIES

My friend Rebecca Shim, a professional chef, feels a deep connection to her grandmother, Elizabettina Polla, who was passionate about every aspect of food—growing, preserving, and cooking it. Although just a teen when her grandma passed away at 86, Rebecca has strong memories of Grandma Bettina, who came from Italy to America at 15, clanging pots and pans in the very early morning as she prepared for holiday feasts. Because Rebecca was young when Grandma Bettina died, no recipe exchanges occurred. Rebecca longed for the recipes her grandmother used to create her delicious Italian cookies, which would arrive a few days before Christmas. Bettina's chocolate spice cookies were one of Rebecca's favorites, and this recipe is an effort to re-create her grandmother's cookie based on childhood memories. Rebecca now includes this cookie with several others in boxes that she parcels out at the holidays, just like Grandma Bettina did.

MAKES 4 DOZEN COOKIES

COOKIES

3 cups all-purpose flour

2/3 cup unsweetened cocoa powder

2 teaspoons baking powder

1 teaspoon baking soda

1 teaspoon salt

1 1/2 teaspoons ground cinnamon

1 teaspoon ground allspice

3/4 teaspoon ground cloves

3/4 teaspoon finely grated nutmeg

8 tablespoons (1 stick) unsalted butter, at room temperature

1 1/4 cups granulated sugar

3 large eggs

2 teaspoons pure vanilla extract

1 cup walnuts, finely chopped

GLAZE

3 cups confectioners' sugar

3 tablespoons unsweetened cocoa powder

1/3 cup milk

1. Preheat the oven to 350°F. Line two baking sheets with parchment paper.

2. Whisk together the flour, cocoa powder, baking powder, baking soda, salt, cinnamon, allspice, cloves, and nutmeg in a bowl.

3. In the bowl of a stand mixer fitted with the paddle attachment, cream the butter and sugar together for 4 minutes. Add the eggs one at a time, beating thoroughly after each addition. Add the vanilla extract and beat again.

4. With the mixer on low, gradually add the dry ingredients and continue beating until fully incorporated. Add the walnuts and stir by hand until just combined.

5. Using a tablespoon measure, make 1-inch round balls with floured fingers and place them 2 inches apart on the prepared baking sheets.

6. Bake for 10 to 12 minutes. The cookies should be firm, but not dry. Do not overbake. Let cool for 5 minutes on the baking sheet before transferring the cookies to a wire rack set over wax paper.

7. Meanwhile, make the glaze: In a small bowl, whisk together the confectioners' sugar, cocoa powder, and milk until smooth.

8. Gently drizzle 1 teaspoon glaze over each cookie. Allow the glaze to set before serving.

BROWN SUGAR GLAZED CARDAMOM CAKE

Cardamom perfumes the halls of our local elementary school when Ann McGillicuddy walks through the doors with her famous cake in hand. She makes it often for bake sales and class functions—a gift to many. Of Finnish descent, Ann is a kindred Scandinavian spirit. She so kindly shared this treasured recipe that was passed down from her grandmother in Finland. This dense, moist cake keeps for days; in fact, the spices deepen and the flavor gets better over time. However, the cake gets eaten so quickly I can't really promise it will last.

SERVES 12

CARDAMOM CAKE

2 1/4 cups all-purpose flour
1 1/2 teaspoons baking powder
1/2 teaspoon salt
1 1/2 teaspoons ground cardamom
1 tablespoon ground cinnamon
3 large eggs, at room temperature
1 3/4 cups granulated sugar
1/2 cup firmly packed light brown sugar
12 tablespoons (1 1/2 sticks) unsalted
   butter, melted
3/4 cup half-and-half
1/2 teaspoon pure vanilla extract

BROWN SUGAR GLAZE

2 cups firmly packed light brown sugar
1/2 cup half-and-half
4 tablespoons unsalted butter
1 teaspoon pure vanilla extract
1 to 2 tablespoons confectioners' sugar
   for dusting (optional)

1. Make the cardamom cake: Preheat the oven to 350°F. Butter and flour a decorative 10-cup bundt pan.

2. In a small bowl, stir together the flour, baking powder, salt, cardamom, and cinnamon. Set aside.

3. In the bowl of a stand mixer fitted with the paddle attachment, beat the eggs and sugars on medium speed until thick and pale yellow in color, about 3 minutes. Add the melted butter and beat on low for about 20 seconds. Add the half-and-half and vanilla extract and beat for another 20 seconds on low, stopping and scraping down the sides of the bowl as necessary with a rubber spatula.

4. Add the dry ingredients and mix well on low for 20 seconds, then increase to medium speed for another 20 seconds.

5. Pour the batter into the prepared pan and bake for 40 to 50 minutes, or until a toothpick inserted into the center of the cake comes out clean. If the top of the cake starts to become a dark brown color after 40 minutes of baking, but the center is not yet set, cover the cake with foil while it finishes baking.

6. Let cool in the bundt pan for 15 minutes; then turn out onto a rack set over wax paper to cool for 1 hour.

7. Meanwhile, make the brown sugar glaze: Place the brown sugar, half-and-half, and butter in a saucepan and cook over medium heat, stirring constantly, until the sugar has dissolved and the mixture just begins to boil. Remove from the heat and stir in the vanilla extract.

8. Slowly drizzle the glaze over the cake, allowing it to run down the sides. Or in lieu of the glaze (which Ann doesn't use), place the confectioners' sugar in a sifter and sprinkle over the cake.

LYNN'S JULEKAKE

Having moved from the Midwest many years ago, I still find myself naturally gravitating toward fellow Scandinavians or their descendants on the East Coast. Perhaps it's a mutual love for a hand knit sweater that starts a conversation, or a desire to cross-country ski. Of course, the language of food is most often where the bond begins. My acquaintance with Lynn Fliegel quickly became a deeper kinship when we realized we were both of Norwegian descent and she insisted we do holiday baking together. She came over with a warm *julekake* in hand (literally "Christmas cake" in Norwegian), and a stack of her grandmother's recipes to share. Lynn, her daughter Jannah, Anna, Camilla, and I baked all afternoon, copying recipes and sharing tales. This cardamom and dried fruit–infused cake always reminds me of that cozy, memorable day. Especially charming is the recipe as Lynn wrote it. The card read, *yulecoga*, which is exactly how Lynn's grandmother pronounced it. Lynn used a phonetic spelling instead of the actual Norwegian spelling, *julekake*. A true example of how recipes evolve. This cake also uses baking powder instead of the yeast used in traditional Norwegian *julekaker*. Perhaps another interpretation somewhere down the line—and a mighty good one. A single bite and I'm sure you'll agree.

SERVES 12 TO 14

8 ounces (2 sticks) unsalted butter,
    at room temperature
2 cups sugar
2 large eggs, at room temperature
5 1/4 cups all-purpose flour
2 teaspoons baking powder
1 teaspoon salt
3 teaspoons ground cardamom
One 12-ounce can evaporated milk
1/3 cup water
1 cup raisins
1/2 cup chopped candied citron

1. Preheat the oven to 350°F. Generously butter and flour a 10- to 12-cup bundt pan.

2. In the bowl of a stand mixer fitted with the paddle attachment, cream the butter and sugar on medium-high until light and fluffy, about 4 minutes. Add the eggs one at a time, beating well after each addition.

3. In a large bowl, stir together the flour, baking powder, salt, and cardamom.

4. In a small bowl, combine the evaporated milk and water.

5. Alternately add the flour and milk mixtures in 5 increments, beginning and ending with the flour.

6. Using a wooden spoon, stir in the raisins and citron.

7. Pour the batter into the prepared pan and bake for 1 hour and 15 minutes. After that time, turn off the oven but keep the cake inside for another 15 minutes. Set on a wire rack to cool for 15 more minutes before gently turning the cake out of the pan.

OLD-FASHIONED GINGERBREAD CAKE

Gingerbread cake is akin to macaroni and cheese in its comfort factor. Everything about it evokes hominess: the pleasingly rich, honey-brown color, the familiar soft texture, and the fragrant, spice-infused aroma—which to me is the scent of the holidays. This moist cake has staying power, which makes it great for gift giving. I like to bake it in a round paper pan, wrap it with an oversized parchment square, and tie it with string for a beautifully nostalgic presentation. To linger over a piece of warm gingerbread cake topped with sweetened whipped cream while snow gently falls outside is like a scene from a storybook, one with a truly sweet ending.

SERVES 12 TO 14

2^1/$_2$ cups all-purpose flour

^{1}/$_2$ teaspoon salt

2 teaspoons ground ginger

1 teaspoon ground cinnamon

^{1}/$_2$ teaspoon ground cloves

^{1}/$_4$ teaspoon freshly grated nutmeg

1^1/$_2$ teaspoons baking soda

1 cup very hot water

8 tablespoons (1 stick) unsalted butter, at room temperature

^{1}/$_2$ cup firmly packed dark brown sugar

1 cup unsulphured dark molasses*

1 large egg

2 teaspoons peeled and grated fresh ginger

1 to 2 tablespoons confectioners' sugar for dusting

* If you spray a glass measuring cup with baking spray prior to measuring the molasses, it slips easily out of the cup without sticking.

1. Preheat the oven to 350°F. Grease a 9-inch round springform or paper pan with baking spray. Line the bottom of the pan with a round of parchment.

2. In a small bowl, stir together the flour, salt, ground ginger, cinnamon, cloves, and nutmeg.

3. In another small bowl, dissolve the baking soda in the very hot water. Set aside.

4. In the bowl of a stand mixer fitted with the paddle attachment, cream the butter and brown sugar for about 3 minutes, stopping and scraping down the sides of the bowl as needed.

5. Add the molasses and mix thoroughly. Add the egg, continuing to mix on medium until fully incorporated. Stir in the fresh ginger. Slowly add the flour mixture and beat on low until fully incorporated, about 40 seconds. Add the baking soda–water mixture. Pulse the mixer a few times on low speed so the water doesn't splash all over, then run at low speed until completely incorporated.

6. Spoon the batter into the prepared pan. Bake for 30 to 35 minutes, or until a toothpick inserted in the center of the cake comes out clean.

7. Let cool completely in the pan. Gently run a knife between the edge of the cake and pan before opening.

8. If desired, place the confectioners' sugar in a sifter and sprinkle over the cake.

PISTACHIO LOVER'S POUND CAKE

Unfailingly for the past 15 years, a tremendously big bag of Bazzini pistachios, sent by one of my husband's clients, has arrived at our door every holiday season. Don't get me wrong, I'm not complaining—I love pistachios. Making your way through five pounds can prove dangerous, though. By early February, I find myself dispensing pistachios to friends, neighbors, and basically anyone who stops by. In order to spread the love and use up the pistachios, I created this Pistachio Pound Cake. Dense and savory with a nutty flavor, it satisfies a pistachio lover's craving, and it's a great way for me to use up my plethora o' pistachios.

SERVES 12

POUND CAKE

8 ounces (2 sticks) unsalted butter
1 cup sugar
1/4 cup honey
3 large eggs
2 cups all-purpose flour
1/3 cup whole milk
1 teaspoon pure vanilla extract
1/2 teaspoon pure almond extract
2/3 cup ground pistachios

PISTACHIO GLAZE

1/2 cup confectioners' sugar
1 tablespoon unsalted butter
2 tablespoons honey
1 tablespoon heavy cream
1/4 cup crushed pistachios

Left: Festively packaged pistachios and the pound cake recipe printed on a decorative card are the perfect accompaniments when gifting this cake for the holidays.

1. Preheat the oven to 325°F. Line a 9 x 5-inch loaf pan with parchment paper, leaving a 1-inch overhang on the two long sides of the pan. Grease the pan and parchment using baking spray.

2. In the bowl of a stand mixer fitted with the paddle attachment, cream the butter, sugar, and honey on medium-high until light and fluffy, about 4 minutes, stopping and scraping down the sides of the bowl as necessary.

3. Add the eggs one at a time, beating well after each addition.

4. Alternately, add the flour and the milk in five parts, beginning and ending with the flour. Beat on medium-high for about 20 seconds between additions, stopping and scraping down the sides of the bowl as necessary. Add the vanilla and almond extracts and the pistachios. Beat on low until combined.

5. Pour the batter into the prepared pan and bake for 1 hour and 30 minutes to 1 hour and 40 minutes, or until cracked on top and a toothpick inserted in the center of the cake comes out clean. After 1 hour of baking (or sooner if needed), cover the cake with aluminum foil to prevent the top from becoming too brown.

6. Let cool in the pan for 10 minutes, then turn out onto a wire rack set over wax paper.

7. Make the pistachio glaze: Combine the confectioners' sugar, butter, honey, and cream in a small saucepan. Cook over medium-low heat, stirring constantly, until the mixture begins to bubble. Continue to cook for 1 more minute while continuing to stir. Remove the glaze from the heat.

8. Slowly spoon the glaze over the top of cake, allowing it to soak in between spoonfuls. Some will run down the sides. Sprinkle the crushed pistachios over the top of the cake and let sit for 1 hour before serving.

POST-IT KAHLÚA CHOCOLATE POUND CAKE

This is the perfect gift to post. My sister, Lisa, developed this recipe for her mother-in-law, Pat, who loved chocolate and Kahlúa—and lived almost 2,000 miles away. Every Christmas season Lisa baked one and shipped it to her cross-country. Upon receipt, Pat would cut the cake into pieces and freeze them individually so she could savor the gift well beyond the holidays.

SERVES 12

1 cup unsweetened cocoa powder

2 cups all-purpose flour

1/2 teaspoon baking powder

1 teaspoon salt

2 tablespoons instant espresso powder

12 ounces (3 sticks) unsalted butter, at room temperature

3 cups sugar

2 teaspoons pure vanilla extract

5 large eggs, at room temperature

1 cup buttermilk

1/4 cup Kahlúa coffee liqueur

Before **GIFT-WRAPPING** the cake, make sure it has **COOLED COMPLETELY**. Place on a cardboard circle. Using a square of **FABRIC** lined with wax paper or **DECORATIVE CELLOPHANE** paper, gather the corners on top of the cake and secure with a **COLORFUL RIBBON**. If you are sending the cake by mail, make sure it is **SEALED COMPLETELY IN PLASTIC WRAP** prior to gift-wrapping. Then carefully place in a shipping box and surround with Styrofoam peanuts. The cake is so moist **IT WILL KEEP FOR DAYS.**

1. Preheat the oven to 325°F. Grease a 15-cup bundt pan using baking spray.

2. Sift together the cocoa powder, flour, baking powder, salt, and espresso powder in a small bowl. Stir several times with a wooden spoon to ensure that the ingredients are evenly distributed.

3. In the bowl of a stand mixer fitted with the paddle attachment, cream the butter on medium for 2 minutes.

4. With the mixer on low, add the sugar in a slow stream. Continue beating on high for 5 minutes, stopping and scraping down the sides of the bowl with a rubber spatula as needed. Slow the mixer and add the vanilla extract. Add the eggs one at a time, beating briefly after each addition. Again stop and scrape down the sides of the bowl as needed.

5. Combine the buttermilk and Kahlúa in a small bowl. Add the dry ingredients alternately with the buttermilk mixture in four increments, beginning and ending with the dry ingredients. Continue stopping and scraping down the sides of the bowl as necessary and blend well.

6. Pour the batter into the prepared pan and bake for about 1 hour and 10 minutes (up to 1 hour and 20 minutes), or until a toothpick inserted in the center of the cake comes out clean.

7. Let the cake cool in the pan for 10 minutes; then unmold onto a wire rack to cool completely.

DECADENT HOT FUDGE SAUCE

A homemade gift in minutes—this ultra-rich sauce is so simple and so sweet. Whip up a batch, make a label for the jar, and pair it with a pint of hand-crafted ice cream. A chocolate lover's dream, this sauce keeps for up to three weeks in the refrigerator. For an even more decadent present, put a jar of caramel sauce in your package too.

MAKES 2 CUPS

One 5-ounce can evaporated milk

12 ounces (about 2 cups) bittersweet
   chocolate 60% cacao pieces or chips

1/4 cup light brown sugar

2 teaspoons pure vanilla extract

2 tablespoons unsalted butter

1. Combine the evaporated milk and chocolate in a saucepan. Cook over medium heat, stirring constantly, until the chocolate is melted, 5 to 7 minutes. Lower the heat and add the brown sugar. Stir until dissolved.

2. Remove from the heat and stir in the vanilla extract and the butter until the butter melts and is thoroughly combined. The sauce will thicken as it cools. It may be reheated on the stovetop until warm or in a microwave oven for 20 to 30 seconds.

NO-FAIL CARAMEL SAUCE

I've tried to cheat and find caramel-making shortcuts that eliminate the time one must stand over the stove, waiting for a clear sugar mixture to turn amber. But alas, similar to many good things worth the effort, there is no time-saving method to be found. You must remain watchful at all times because this sauce can turn hard as a rock in the blink of an eye. Otherwise creamy and smooth, it is the perfect topping for ice cream, pie, or fruit. When packaged in a glass jar, the ravishing amber sauce makes a tantalizing gift. Be sure to add a tag with refrigeration (up to 3 weeks) and reheating instructions.

MAKES 2 1/2 CUPS

1/2 cup water

2 cups sugar

1 tablespoon light corn syrup

8 tablespoons (1 stick) unsalted butter,
   cut into 1/2-inch pieces

1 cup heavy cream, at room temperature

Pinch of salt

1. Combine the water, sugar, and corn syrup in a heavy 3-quart saucepan. Cook over medium-high heat without boiling until the sugar dissolves and the mixture becomes clear.

2. Once the sugar is dissolved, let the sauce come to a boil. Lower the heat and gently boil, without stirring, until the edges become light brown, about 20 minutes. Swirl the pan to blend the darker mixture with the light and cook over medium-high heat, still only swirling, until the sauce becomes amber—this could happen in a matter of seconds or up to 10 minutes, so watch carefully. Do not let the sauce become brown or red or it will burn.

3. Remove from the heat and add the butter. Use a wooden spoon to stir until completely melted. Add the heavy cream and salt while continuing to stir quickly. If the sauce lumps up, continue to stir vigorously. If needed, place the mixture back over low heat and stir until smooth and creamy. Reheat the sauce using a double-boiler or with low heat in a microwave.

BEST BRAN MUFFINS

Instead of socks, beverage napkins, or candles, give a gift with meaning. One birthday I received a bran muffin recipe from my aunt Susie, and with it came a devotion recounting humble beginnings, "…our food budget as newlyweds in England was $10 per week. We ate a lot of bran muffins, macaroni and cheese, and granary bread back then because they were all cheap." Susie went on to tell how material possessions became enslaving and how she prayed for contentment and found it. "Now I look at my life, which is so totally different than it once was, and I realize what true contentment is…eating vegetables that I grow myself, conserving the Earth's precious resources…and contentment comes from bran muffins…having the time to make them, and having a child who gobbles up every last crumb." I am grateful for what she shared with me: a recipe and a story, a piece of her life. Consider giving a friend or family member a recipe with special meaning, and send it with an account of its significance. Meaningful gifts are memorable.

MAKES 12 MUFFINS

2 cups 100% bran cereal, such as Kellogg's All-Bran

1 1/4 cups milk

1 large egg, lightly beaten

1/4 cup canola or vegetable oil

1/3 cup dark firmly packed brown sugar

3 tablespoons honey

1 tablespoon baking powder

1/2 teaspoon salt

1/3 cup granola cereal such as Cascadian Farms Fruit and Nut Granola

1/4 cup old-fashioned rolled oats

2/3 cup whole wheat flour

1 cup fresh blueberries

1. Preheat the oven to 400°F. Line a standard 12-cup muffin tin with paper liners.

2. In a large mixing bowl, combine the bran cereal and milk. Let stand for several minutes to let the cereal soften.

3. Add the egg and oil and stir until combined. Add the brown sugar, honey, baking powder, and salt. Stir until thoroughly mixed. Stir in the granola and oats. Add the flour and mix until just combined. Fold in the blueberries.

4. Spoon the batter into the prepared pan. Bake for 20 minutes, or until a toothpick inserted in the center of a muffin comes out clean.

SINFUL CINNAMON ROLLS

Yeast rolls are one of my grandmother's specialties. She turns out dozens at a time. Her dough is versatile—she uses it for buttery, pillowy-soft, perfectly browned dinner rolls and for sweet, scrumptious cinnamon rolls. Although well worth it, an ample effort is required to make these rolls. Then one day I came across a recipe that uses a bread machine. Bingo! I dumped the ingredients in the machine and walked away. Two hours and thirty minutes later my dough was done. These rolls can be assembled the night before and kept refrigerated in the pan. Simply wake up and bake. The large, sinfully sweet, gooey buns fresh from the oven are the perfect morning greeting to any overnight guest.

MAKES 16 ROLLS
DOUGH

1/4 cup very warm water

1 teaspoon plus 1/2 cup granulated sugar

1 enevlope (21/4 teaspoons) dry active
   yeast

1 cup whole milk

8 tablespoons (1 stick) unsalted butter

1/2 teaspoon salt

1 large egg, lightly beaten

11/2 teaspoons pure vanilla extract

41/2 cups unbleached white bread flour

1 tablespoon vital wheat gluten

FILLING

2/3 cup firmly packed dark brown sugar

3 tablespoons ground cinnamon

6 tablespoons unsalted butter,
   at room temperature

FROSTING

3 ounces cream cheese,
   at room temperature

6 tablespoons unsalted butter,
   at room temperature

11/2 cups confectioners' sugar

1 teaspoon pure vanilla extract

1. Make the dough: If using a bread maker: Put all the ingredients in a 11/2- to 2-pound bread maker according to the manufacturer's instructions with the following two changes: (1) Melt the butter and add with the liquid ingredients. (2) Replace the water with milk. Run the bread maker on the dough setting and when finished, turn out the dough onto a floured surface and skip to step 7.

2. If not using a bread maker: Butter a large glass or ceramic bowl in which the dough will rise.

3. Put the water in a bowl and add 1 teaspoon of the granulated sugar. Stir to dissolve. Sprinkle with the yeast, stir again to dissolve, and let stand for 5 minutes, or until frothy.

4. Put the milk in a saucepan and cook over medium heat until it begins to steam and bubble slightly on the edges. Lower the heat and add the butter, remaining 1/2 cup granulated sugar, and the salt. Stir until the butter is melted and the sugar is dissolved. Remove from the heat and let cool.

5. When the milk mixture has cooled, add the proofed yeast mixture, egg, and vanilla extract and stir. Add the flour and vital wheat gluten and continue to stir until smooth.

6. Turn the dough out onto a floured surface and knead for several minutes until soft. Sprinkle flour over the dough if it's sticky and knead a few more times. Place in the prepared bowl, cover, and set in a warm place to rise until doubled in size, about 1 hour. Punch it down and turn it out onto a lightly floured surface.

7. Grease two 8-inch square pans with baking spray.

8. Make the filling: In a small bowl, combine the brown sugar and cinnamon. Stir until thoroughly combined.

9. Using a rolling pin, form the dough into a 16- x 24-inch rectangle. With a rubber spatula or knife, spread the butter gently

over the entire rectangle of dough, leaving a 1-inch margin at the top long edge of the dough. Sprinkle the cinnamon mixture on top, avoiding the 1-inch margin at the top (you don't want to butter or sugar the edge that will be used to seal the dough).

10. Starting with the bottom long edge of the rectangle, roll the dough tightly away from you toward the top. When you reach the top, press the clean edge into the rolled dough to seal. Using a sharp knife, cut the rolled dough into 1- to 1½-inch sections. You should get 16 rolls. Place the rolls around the edges of the prepared pan (8 to a pan). Cover the two pans with dish towels and let rise a second time, about 30 minutes.

11. Preheat the oven to 350°F. Bake the risen rolls for 15 to 20 minutes, or until lightly browned.

12. Make the frosting: In the bowl of an electric mixer fitted with the paddle attachment, combine the cream cheese and butter. Beat for 6 minutes, or until light and fluffy. Gradually add the confectioners' sugar and beat for another 3 minutes, or until fluffy again. Add the vanilla extract and beat until blended.

13. Divide the frosting between the two pans, liberally spreading it across the top of the rolls as soon as they come out of the oven. Let cool for several minutes before eating.

JEANNE'S BLUEBERRY PIE

Henry Higginson sounds like a fictional character, but he's not. He's an elderly gentleman who missed the bus home after spending a day at the library. He lived over a hundred miles away and it would be hours before the next bus arrived. Jeanne Kiel was working at the reference desk and, because the library was closing for the night, offered her home as a place of respite while he waited for the next bus. Jeanne and her husband learned that the man had no family—and loved blueberry pie. Jeanne quickly went to work while her husband entertained the man. She just made the deadline of the next bus's departure, and handed Mr. Higginson a warm pie to sweeten his journey.

Several weeks later, the mailman delivered a very special letter to Jeanne—a shakily handwritten note expressing Mr. Higginson's gratitude for "the best pie ever," plus a ten dollar bill. Thirty-five years later, the touching gesture of note and ten dollars still remains in Jeanne's safe deposit box, a reminder of a gentle, kind man so appreciative of a simple gift of friendship.

SERVES 8 TO 10

5 cups fresh blueberries

2/3 cup sugar

1/3 cup all-purpose flour

2 teaspoons freshly squeezed lemon juice

1 batch Flaky Pie Crust Dough (page 11)

2 tablespoons unsalted butter, cut into
   1/2-inch pieces

1. Stir the berries, sugar, flour, and lemon juice together in a large bowl. Set aside.

2. Preheat the oven to 425°F.

3. On a lightly floured surface, roll the first disk of dough out to form a 12-inch circle. Place in a 9-inch pie plate. Roll out the second disk into an 11-inch circle.

4. Spoon the filling into the crust and dot with the butter. Cover the filling with the second dough circle. Seal the top dough edge to the bottom edge by wrapping the top under the bottom edge and crimping. Make a decorative edge if desired. Using a knife, make several vents in the top crust.

5. Place the pie plate on an aluminun foil–covered baking sheet and bake for 50 minutes, or until the crust is a light golden color. To prevent the edges of the crust from burning, place a pie shield over them or cover with foil when baking and remove for the last 25 minutes of baking.

6. Let the pie cool for 1 hour before serving.

SECRET-INGREDIENT VANILLA CUPCAKES

"What's in these?" I asked Judith Bromley after taking a bite of an exceptionally tasty cupcake she had made. "Coconut milk," she replied. "I use it as a substitute all the time." I had to give it a try. I replaced cow's milk with coconut in my vanilla cupcake recipe, and I'm not kidding, I got the same exclamation from my neighbor when she tried one: "What's in these?" she asked me.

Once you make these cupcakes, you'll swear off box mixes forever. They're so easy—they take about ten minutes to stir up—and prompt such a great response. I like to make them as mini cupcakes; the two-bite size (perhaps one for some) is perfect for kids' parties or social functions. The cake crumb is tender yet moist, and the perfect base for the creamy white frosting that also uses the secret ingredient.

MAKES 48 MINI OR 24 STANDARD CUPCAKES

1 3/4 cups all-purpose flour

2 1/2 teaspoons baking powder

8 tablespoons (1 stick) unsalted butter, at room temperature

1 cup sugar

3 large eggs, at room temperature

2/3 cup unsweetened coconut milk

2 teaspoons pure vanilla extract

SECRET-INGREDIENT FROSTING

12 tablespoons (1 1/2 sticks) unsalted butter, at room temperature

6 cups confectioners' sugar

1/2 cup unsweetened coconut milk

1/2 teaspoon pure vanilla extract

1. Make the cupcakes: Preheat the oven to 350°F. Line 2 mini or standard cupcake pans with paper liners.

2. Stir together the flour and baking powder in a small bowl.

3. Combine the butter and sugar in the bowl of a stand mixer fitted with the paddle attachment. Cream for 3 minutes on high until light and fluffy, stopping and scraping down the sides of the bowl with a rubber spatula as needed.

4. Add the eggs one at a time, beating well after each addition. Add the coconut milk and flour mixture alternately, beginning and ending with the flour. Beat well after each addition, for about 20 seconds, making sure the ingredients are thoroughly combined, again stopping and scraping down the sides of the bowl as needed. Stir in the vanilla extract.

5. Spoon the batter into the prepared pans. Bake the mini cupcakes for 12 minutes, or until a toothpick inserted into a cupcake comes out clean. The edges of the cupcakes will begin to turn a pale golden but the tops of the cupcakes will be pale. Do not overbake. (If making standard-size cupcakes, bake for 15 to 18 minutes.) Remove from the oven and let cool on a rack.

6. Make the secret-ingredient frosting: Put the butter in the bowl of the stand mixer fitted with the paddle attachment and beat for 2 minutes. Add the confectioners' sugar and mix until thoroughly combined. Pour in the coconut milk and vanilla extract and beat until smooth and creamy. Use to frost the cooled cupcakes.

CREATING

Every man has a history worth knowing,
if he could tell it, or we could draw it from him.

—RALPH WALDO EMERSON

When we share food and conversation, good times and laughs, we are creating memories that will become part of our own personal histories. My husband and I have spent some of our most treasured times together with food. When I was six months pregnant with Anna, we traveled to the Dordogne region of France for a wedding. With a baby on the way, we knew this would be our last big hurrah for a while. The entire trip was culinary-based: visits to foie gras farms, truffle tours, and long, lavish meals with friends. Each moment and each bite was memorable. We tease that the trip gave Anna a taste for the finer things, but nonetheless we never cheat our kids out of a good meal; we encourage them by including them in seven-course dinners and other epicurean adventures.

Since both girls were born, they have been in the kitchen while we cooked (strapped in their baby carriers on the counter watching). As soon as they could hold spoons, we had them mixing and measuring. Because we involve Anna and Camilla in the cooking and baking processes, they are interested in the end result, and always willing and wanting to try new and different things.

When we travel as a family, we eat locally and come home to re-create our finds. We involve the girls and discuss ingredients: "Do you think it was almond or pistachio?" or "What type of chocolate do you think they used, milk or dark?"

Spending time in the kitchen with family and friends is important to us. It's how we share places we've discovered, experience new ideas, and get downright creative. I believe food can break down barriers between people and change the way people see things—and each other.

CREATING HISTORY WITH RECIPES

Creating your own history with recipes is as important as preserving recipes from the past. For those who don't have a family story rich with recipes, this is your opportunity to begin one. Recipes you archive will impart clues about you and your family to future generations. Recipes can allude to travel, document experiences, and reveal friends and acquaintances. Your tastes and preferences will also be conveyed.

You may notice that the recipes in this chapter are slightly different than the ones in the first chapter. Most of the Preserving recipes are made with easy-to-find ingredients and don't have sophisticated flavor combinations. Just like the times from which many of those recipes came, the desserts are simple and straightforward. My great-grandmother's recipes were based around flour, butter or lard, sugar, eggs, vanilla, and baking powder with some fruit, nuts, or cocoa powder for flavoring.

In this chapter you'll see the influence globalization has had on my Midwestern palate: dulce de leche, passion fruit, cacao nibs, and fromage blanc. These tastes would have been exotic to my Northern European ancestors—to them, garlic was spicy. I have documented these developments in my own recipe notes so my descendants will understand how the world has changed.

Some people I meet say they have no traditions. I always find it hard to believe and start asking questions. Eventually, after some probing, they realize that, in fact, they have many! Even something that seems as unexceptional as going out for ice cream with the family every Sunday after dinner is exceptional. It's something you do together with your family. It's a tradition, and it's an event that brings you together.

CREATING YOUR OWN FOOD STORY

While your life story will be made up of thousands of memories, I can almost guarantee that at least a few will be summoned by food. Here are some ideas for creating your own food story:

1. **TAKE A BAKING CLASS** Many community colleges and local restaurants offer one-time classes that focus on learning to make a single item, such as a specific type of cookie or cake. Baking with a pro may inspire you.

2. **BAKE WITH FRIENDS** If you admire a friend's baking skills, ask that person to show you his or her techniques; it's a constructive way to spend time together.

3. **START YOUR OWN ARCHIVE** It's important to maintain a record of your recipes, where you get them, what inspires you. Consider keeping a journal or three-ring binder of your favorites.

4. **USE PRESERVING IDEAS IN CHAPTER 1 TO DOCUMENT THE PRESENT** While it's wonderful to preserve the past, there's no time like now to document family members in the kitchen. Videotape your twenty-something cousin who just brought back a new recipe from his trip abroad, or document the uncle who just got a new Big Green Egg grill. (Your documentation could help future generations grill on the Egg!)

5. **CREATE AN ANNUAL COOKIE OR RECIPE EXCHANGE** Don't put it off another year, start a cookie exchange now. It's a social event with the added benefit of acquiring recipes, trying new foods, and learning others' traditions. There are many online sources and books, such as Lauren Chattman's *Cookie Swap*!

6. **TAKE A TRIP TO LEARN ABOUT FOOD YOU'RE INTERESTED IN** If you're in search of your grandmother's Italian cookie recipe, research the area she came from and plan a trip there. Try to set up a visit in advance with a local baker or restaurateur. Explain your quest and the information you'd like to unearth.

7. **KEEP LISTS OF CELEBRATORY MENUS AND RECIPES** Dedicate a book or journal solely to holiday menus and recipes. Such records will reveal much to future generations while helping current kin maintain traditions.

8. **START A FAMILY COLLECTION** Begin a tradition of collecting one particular item, such as silver spoons, cookie cutters, or cake servers. Family members will work together to build the collection, which will provide common inspiration. Break out and use the collection when everyone is gathered, and display it at other times for a fond reminder of the times spent together.

9. **USE A CHERISHED RECIPE FOR A SPECIAL DAY** Create a new annual ritual using your favorite recipe. If your family loves your hot cross buns but you only make them once every blue moon, commit to making them every Easter, so your family can eagerly anticipate the baked treat every year.

10. **CELEBRATE WEEKLY** No need to wait for special occasions to bake—designate one evening a week as cookie or cupcake night. Just as some families may eat pizza on Wednesdays or fish on Fridays, bake together at a defined time. By trying new recipes, you'll learn, laugh, and grow together.

INDIVIDUAL RUSTIC CARAMEL APPLE TARTLETS

⧗

Some years ago, while eating breakfast at my friend Heidi's house, she set an open can on the table. There was no label and a spoon stuck upright in the caramel-colored contents. Heidi's daughter coated her toast with the thick, creamy spread. Not knowing what to expect, my daughters and I followed suit. Oh, am I glad I did. It was her Cuban mother's dulce de leche, which Heidi makes four or five cans of at a time by simmering cans of sweetened condensed milk in water on the stovetop for several hours. Now dulce de leche is available in many places. Upscale brands like Argentina's La Salamandra are sold online and in specialty markets; Nestle's La Lechera is sold in most US supermarkets. Even the Girl Scouts sell dulce de leche cookies. I, too, have caught the wave and use this milk-based caramel sauce when and where I can, like on these rustic apple tartlets, which are the perfect accompaniment to the habit-forming sauce.

MAKES SIX 5-INCH TARTLETS

1^1/2 pounds Granny Smith apples,
    peeled, cored, thinly sliced, and cut
    into 1-inch pieces (about 3^1/4 cups)
1 tablespoon all-purpose flour
2 tablespoons light brown sugar
^{1}/4 teaspoon salt
^{1}/4 teaspoon ground cinnamon
^{1}/4 teaspoon freshly grated nutmeg
1 teaspoon grated lemon zest
2 teaspoons lemon juice
1 vanilla bean
1 batch Flaky Pie Crust Dough (page 11)
2 tablespoons unsalted butter,
    cut into 6 cubes
^{1}/2 cup dulce de leche
Dulce de leche and Camilla Vanilla
    ice creams (pages 130 and 131)

1. Stir together the apples, flour, brown sugar, salt, cinnamon, nutmeg, lemon zest, and lemon juice.

2. Split the vanilla bean lengthwise with a knife and scrape the seeds into the apple mixture. Set aside.

3. Line a baking sheet with parchment paper.

4. Divide the dough into 6 parts. Roll each part out into a 6-inch circle. Place the dough circles on the prepared baking sheet. Place 2/3 cup filling in the center of each dough circle, leaving a 1/2-inch border. Dot each mound of filling with one butter cube. Carefully lift the dough up to enclose the edges of the apple mounds, pleating the dough as you encircle the center mounds. Chill the filled tartlets for 1 hour.

5. Preheat the oven to 450°F.

6. Bake the chilled tartlets for 20 to 25 minutes, or until the apples are tender and the crust is golden brown.

7. Meanwhile, heat the dulce de leche over medium heat until warm.

8. Remove the tartlets from the oven and drizzle with warm dulce de leche. Let the tartlets stand for 10 minutes before serving, or serve at room temperature. Serve with the ice creams.

DULCE DE LECHE ICE CREAM

The ultimate expression for dulce de leche: ice cream. When frozen, it becomes even creamier, smoother, and more satisfying (I think because it seems less sweet, you can eat more of it!). Dole out a big scoop of this ice cream with each Rustic Apple Tartlet on page 128, or serve it alone. This ice cream has no problem standing on its own.

MAKES 1¹/₂ QUARTS

3¹/2 cups whole milk

6 large egg yolks

1 cup dulce de leche, such as
   La Salamandra brand

¹/4 cup heavy cream

¹/4 teaspoon pure vanilla extract

1. Pour the milk into a saucepan and cook over medium heat until it begins to steam and bubble around the edges. Do not let boil.

2. When the milk is steamy, add the egg yolks and continue to cook for another 6 minutes over low heat, whisking constantly.

3. Remove from the heat and add the dulce de leche, whisking until it's dissolved. Stir in the cream and vanilla extract.

4. Let cool to room temperature, then chill in the refrigerator for 2 hours.

5. Freeze in an ice cream maker according to the manufacturer's instructions.

CAMILLA VANILLA ICE CREAM ⧗

The nine-year-old Camilla writes: "Even though people think vanilla is a plain ice cream flavor, it's my favorite. The beauty of vanilla is that it's a simple flavor so any toppings work (my favorite is hot fudge). It's delicious with dessert and it's bursting with a flavor that melts in your mouth. I like homemade vanilla ice cream the best because I find it creamier, and [it has] more of a vanilla flavor. I hope you'll enjoy it as much as I do!"

MAKES 1 QUART

3 large egg yolks

3/4 cup sugar

11/2 cups whole milk

1 vanilla bean

11/2 cups heavy cream

1 teaspoon pure vanilla extract

1. In a small bowl, whisk together the egg yolks and sugar. The mixture will be grainy and thick. Set aside.

2. Pour the milk into a heavy saucepan. Split the vanilla bean lengthwise and scrape the seeds into the milk. Put the scraped bean in the milk too.

3. Place the saucepan over medium heat and whisk occasionally until it begins to steam and bubbles start to appear. Do not let boil.

4. Turn the heat to low and add the yolk mixture, whisking constantly for 4 minutes. Switch to a wooden spoon and cook for another 3 minutes, stirring constantly.

5. Remove from the heat and stir in the cream and vanilla extract. Let cool to room temperature, then chill in the refrigerator for at least 2 hours.

6. Remove the vanilla bean and freeze in an ice cream maker according to the manufacturer's instructions.

APPLE CRISP AND CREAM PARFAITS

I have several toothsome apple crisp recipes, including one from my mother, but this one is my fave. It comes from my good friend Chelsea Mauldin, who, just like this crisp, is dependable, comforting, and a true classic. I say the crisp is dependable because it always turns out tasty (this is a very forgiving recipe). The silky cream paired with the satisfying crisp makes it comforting, and the pure apple-and-oat flavor makes it a classic—no bells, no whistles, no hard-to-find ingredients here. The only thing you may not have is a parfait glass. In that case, use any 8-ounce glass. Even a juice glass can be dressed up for dessert. I love serving these parfaits at dinner parties. I assemble them right before guests arrive. If you prefer the crisp warm, enlist a guest to help you put them together right before the last course. As for Chelsea, my thanks go to her for being as reliable as this crisp!

MAKES 8 TO 10 PARFAITS
FILLING

5 medium (about 2 1/2 pounds) Granny Smith apples, peeled, cored, and cut into 3/4-inch dice (about 6 cups)
1/4 cup firmly packed light brown sugar
1/2 teaspoon ground cinnamon
1 tablespoon all-purpose flour
1/2 teaspoon freshly grated nutmeg
1 tablespoon lemon juice

TOPPING

1 cup all-purpose flour
1 cup old-fashioned rolled oats
1 cup firmly packed light brown sugar
1/4 teaspoon salt
8 tablespoons (1 stick) unsalted butter, at room temperature

WHIPPED CREAM

2 cups heavy cream
3 tablespoons confectioners' sugar
1 teaspoon pure vanilla extract

1. Preheat the oven to 375°F. Butter a 9 x 13-inch baking dish.

2. Make the filling: In a medium bowl, toss the apples with the brown sugar, cinnamon, flour, nutmeg, and lemon juice. Set aside.

3. Make the topping: Put the flour, oats, brown sugar, and salt in a bowl and stir.

4. Cut the butter into 1-inch pieces and add it to the flour mixture. Using a pastry blender or two forks, mix together until small clumps appear. Then gently squeeze the topping mixture in the bowl with your fingers to create some large clumps.

5. Spread the filling in the bottom of the prepared baking dish. Put the large clumps of topping over the filling and spread the rest of the loose topping evenly over the entire surface of the fruit.

6. Bake for 35 to 40 minutes, or until the fruit is bubbling and the topping is crisp and browned. At this point, you can serve it as is, scooping out spoonfuls into bowls, or move on to step 7.

7. Make the whipped cream: In the chilled bowl of a stand mixer fitted with the whisk attachment, beat the cream until stiff. Stir in the confectioners' sugar and vanilla extract.

8. To assemble the parfaits, scoop two spoonfuls of crisp into an 8-ounce parfait or juice glass. Top with a large spoonful of whipped cream. Repeat until there are 3 layers total of both the crisp and cream, starting with the crisp and ending with the cream. There should be enough crisp and cream to make 8 to 10 parfaits.

CHOCOLATE LEAF PUMPKIN BARS

While I confess that I find the predictably of pumpkin pie somewhat tiresome, I really do love the familiar flavor. It's an old standby that I take for granted. Fall without pumpkin pie would be like the season without changing leaves. Perhaps that's why I like these bars so much. The well-known spice blend is present like an old friend, yet an unexpected chocolate crust and topping add variety—plus the dark, shiny chocolate leaves give the presentation flair. Because of their portability and easy prep (even the leaves, which are a great project for kids, are quick to make), these bars are excellent for group meetings and family gatherings.

MAKES 48 BARS

CRUST

One 9-ounce package Famous Chocolate
   Wafer cookies (yields about 2 1/4 cups
   cookie crumbs)
1/4 cup sugar
6 tablespoons unsalted butter, melted

FILLING

One 8-ounce package cream cheese
One 15-ounce can pumpkin puree
One 14-ounce can sweetened
   condensed milk
2 large eggs
1 teaspoon pure vanilla extract
1 teaspoon ground cinnamon
1 teaspoon ground ginger
1/4 teaspoon ground allspice
1/2 teaspoon freshly grated nutmeg
1/4 teaspoon ground cloves

TOPPING

1 cup semisweet chocolate chips
Nontoxic leaves, such as unsprayed rose

1. Preheat the oven to 350°F. Grease a 9 x 13-inch baking pan with baking spray.

2. Make the crust: Use a food processer to turn the cookies into fine crumbs. Add the sugar and combine. Sprinkle the melted butter evenly over and process until the crumbs are moistened. Press the crumbs evenly into the prepared baking pan using an offset spatula. Bake the crust for 8 minutes, then remove from the oven. Increase the oven temperature to 400°F.

3. Make the filling: Using the food processor, whip the cream cheese until light and fluffy, about 2 minutes. Add the pumpkin, sweetened condensed milk, eggs, and vanilla extract. Process 1 minute, until thoroughly combined. Add the cinnamon, ginger, allspice, nutmeg, and cloves. Process until fully incorporated.

4. Pour the filling over the baked crust and bake for 10 minutes at 400°F. Lower the oven temperature to 350°F and bake for another 35 to 40 minutes, or until the center is set and a knife inserted in the center comes out clean. Let cool on a wire rack.

5. Make the topping: Heat the chocolate in a double boiler over medium heat until melted, stirring constantly. Let cool to lukewarm. Put 1/2 cup in a plastic baggie, squeeze to one corner, snip off a tiny bit of the corner of the bag, and squeeze the chocolate out over the bars in a cross-hatch pattern. After the topping has hardened, cut the bars into 1 1/2-inch squares.

6. Use the remaining chocolate for making chocolate leaves: Using a pastry brush, cover the back of the leaves with the melted chocolate. Place on a wax paper–covered baking sheet. Refrigerate until firm, about 10 minutes.

7. Remove from the refrigerator, gently peel off the green leaf, and a molded chocolate leaf will remain. Place 1 on each pumpkin bar.

CREAMY RICE PUDDING

A friend invited me for a simple Sunday supper in Norway and it was there I ate my first Norwegian *risengøt* (rice porridge) as a main course. Many cultures include some form of rice pudding as a traditional menu item. In India it may be cooked with coconut milk and in Southeast Asia they may use black rice, but the idea is the same: sweetened, thickened, slow-cooked rice. In our family we like this creamy, comforting pudding for dessert. We haven't tried it for dinner yet—although one could justify eating rice pudding for dinner; after all, rice is one of the world's most important grains. Maybe we need to take note from the Scandinavians and reconsider rice pudding's place.

SERVES 6

4 1/4 cups whole milk, plus more
   if necessary
1/4 cup sugar
1/4 teaspoon salt
2/3 cup jasmine rice
1/2 teaspoon pure vanilla extract
2 tablespoons slivered almonds (optional)
Ground cinnamon for sprinkling
   (optional)

1. Combine the milk, sugar, and salt in a heavy-bottomed saucepan over medium heat and bring to a gentle boil.

2. Turn down the heat to low and add the rice. Simmer, uncovered, for 30 to 45 minutes, stirring occasionally as it thickens.

3. When the rice is softened and the pudding has thickened, stir in the vanilla extract. (If the rice is not softened, but the pudding is thick, add 1 or 2 tablespoons more milk and cook until the desired consistency is achieved.)

4. Divide the pudding among bowls, sprinkle with the almonds and cinnamon, if desired, and serve.

ANNA BANANA MUFFINS

Formerly Hannah Banana Bread, this recipe, given to me by a former colleague, was renamed Anna Banana Muffins for our daughter, who gobbles up these sweet, healthy treats on Saturday mornings. (You can still use this recipe to make bread, but mini muffins are more manageable for little fingers.) I make them almost weekly. It's a great way to use overripe bananas—the mushier the better. I like to keep some muffins in the freezer for unexpected guests. Packed with fiber, these no-fail muffins are sure to become a family favorite. Muffins may be frozen in a Ziploc bag and defrosted individually for approximately 30 seconds in a microwave.

MAKES 24 MINI MUFFINS

1/2 cup safflower oil

1 cup firmly packed light brown sugar

2 large eggs

1 teaspoon pure vanilla extract

3 medium-size ripe bananas, cut into
   small pieces, plus 1 banana sliced
   into 24 thin slices (optional)

1 1/2 cups whole wheat flour

1/2 cup wheat germ

2 teaspoons baking powder

1/2 teaspoon salt

1/2 teaspoon ground cinnamon

1. Preheat the oven to 350°F. Grease a 24-cup mini muffin pan using baking spray.

2. Cream the oil and brown sugar together in the bowl of a stand mixer fitted with the paddle attachment until smooth and moist.

3. With the mixer on low, add the eggs one at a time until fully incorporated. Stir in the vanilla extract.

4. With the mixer on low, add the bananas and mix until the batter is smooth and most of the banana is pureed. Stir in the flour, wheat germ, baking powder, salt, and cinnamon and beat on low until moistened. Do not overbeat.

5. Using a tablespoon or ice cream scoop, fill the prepared muffin cups. If desired, place 1 slice of banana on top of the batter in each muffin cup. Bake for 15 to 20 minutes, or until a toothpick inserted into a muffin comes out clean.

6. Let the muffins cool in the pan.

SUGARED MANGO MUFFINS

Saturday mornings spent at home call for big breakfasts. Still in our pajamas, we take time to prepare dishes that weekday schedules prohibit: Belgian waffles, baked eggs, and muffins. My family loves muffins, and our favorites are the ones laden with sweet, ripe fruit—blueberries, raspberries, peaches. While I prefer this recipe with mango, you can substitute any of the aforementioned fruits. Although usually available year round, mangoes are at their best in spring and summer, which is when I bake these moist muffins that aren't too dense and deliver the essence of mango. These muffins are best eaten the day they are baked.

MAKES 16 TO 18 MUFFINS

1 3/4 cups all-purpose flour

1/2 teaspoon salt

1 teaspoon baking powder

1/4 teaspoon baking soda

6 tablespoons unsalted butter, at room temperature

1 cup granulated sugar

2 large eggs, at room temperature

1 teaspoon pure vanilla extract

1/2 cup sour cream

2 to 3 mangoes, cut into 3/4-inch dice (about 1 1/2 cups)

2 tablespoons sparkling white sugar or coarse sugar crystals

1. Preheat the oven to 350°F. Place paper liners in 18 standard muffin cups.

2. Sift together the flour, salt, baking powder, and baking soda in a medium bowl. Set aside.

3. Put the butter and granulated sugar in the bowl of a stand mixer fitted with the paddle attachment and cream together on medium for 3 minutes. Add the eggs one at a time, blending each time until fully incorporated, stopping and scraping down the sides of the bowl as needed with a rubber spatula. Stir in the vanilla extract.

4. With the mixer on low, slowly add half of the dry ingredients. Using a rubber spatula, stop and scrape the sides of the bowl to ensure everything is moistened.

5. Add the sour cream and beat until just combined. With the mixer on low, add the rest of the dry ingredients until moistened, stopping and scraping down the sides of the bowl with the spatula. Do not overbeat. Stir in the mangoes using the spatula or a wooden spoon.

6. Using a tablespoon or ice cream scoop, fill the prepared muffin cups three-quarters full. Sprinkle each muffin with 1/4 teaspoon sparkling sugar.

7. Bake for 18 to 20 minutes, or until pale golden and a toothpick inserted into a muffin comes out clean. Let cool in the pan.

Left: Sugared Mango Muffins
Right: Anna Banana Muffins

PASSION FRUIT BREAD PUDDING

Inspired by the dessert menu at Jake's Resort in Jamaica, this Passion Fruit Bread Pudding will transport you to the Caribbean with one bite. Jamaica's southern coast, known as the Breadbasket, provides the resort, which serves only island-grown fruit, with loads of local produce. You never know what you may find on the daily changing menu of the resort's Jack Sprat restaurant. Handwritten on a chalkboard visible from the pool area, the enticing choices lure guests all day. Always listed are several ice cream and dessert options incorporating mangoes, passion fruit, papaya, and other island fruit. While there, we indulged in dessert with every meal—the bread pudding was one of my favorites. If you serve it with passion fruit sauce and homemade Toasted Coconut Ice Cream (see opposite page), you may just hear the waves lapping Jamaica's shore.

SERVES 12

BREAD PUDDING

One 12-ounce loaf country white bread,
   cut into 1-inch cubes (about 8 cups)
2 tablespoons unsalted butter, melted
1 cup passion fruit pulp or puree*
1 cup sugar
6 large egg yolks
1 cup half-and-half
1 cup unsweetened coconut milk

SAUCE

1/2 cup passion fruit puree
1/3 cup sugar
3 tablespoons heavy cream

* Goya Passion Fruit Pulp is available
  in the frozen food section of many
  markets. Also try specialty Latin
  American grocers for passion fruit
  puree.

1. Preheat the oven to 350°F. Butter a 9 x 13-inch glass baking dish.

2. Put the bread cubes on a baking sheet and sprinkle with the melted butter. Toss well. Bake for 12 minutes; remove from the oven.

3. Meanwhile, combine the passion fruit pulp, sugar, and egg yolks in a saucepan and cook over medium-low heat until slightly thickened, about 10 minutes.

4. Stir in the half-and-half and coconut milk and raise the heat to medium. Cook until the mixture comes to a gentle simmer, then continue cooking for another 2 minutes. Remove from the heat.

5. Place the bread cubes in the prepared baking dish and pour the passion fruit mixture evenly over them. Press the cubes down gently with the back of an offset spatula to ensure that the liquid completely covers them. Let stand for 30 minutes.

6. Preheat the oven to 350°F.

7. Bake the pudding for 35 minutes, or until the edges of some of the bread cubes start to turn slightly golden brown. Remove from the oven.

8. Make the sauce: Combine all the ingredients together in a small saucepan and heat over medium until the mixture comes to a slow boil. Continue to stir and gently boil for 15 minutes, until the sauce is thickened and reduced by one-fourth.

9. Serve each scoop of the warm bread pudding with 1 tablespoon of sauce.

TOASTED COCONUT ICE CREAM

Before the plethora of today's artisanal ice cream shops, good ice cream had to be sought out. An ice-cream junkie, I have spent hours searching for specialty shops that dispense the real McCoy—no national, big-batch brands accepted. From Malaysia to Maine, I have found those spots and can most likely tell you where they sell ice cream in any town I've been. The ones that stand out are the Pelangi Lounge Bar in Langkawi that serves up cool, refreshing desserts with red bean and grass jelly, a novelty to my Western palate; my husband introduced me to Grape Nuts ice cream at the family-run Bummel's (now a Gifford's) in Waterville, Maine; and the green tea ice cream at Manhattan's Chinatown Ice Cream Factory is not to be missed.

Jenny's Ice Cream in Williamsville, New York, though, has an especially sweet spot in my heart. It was at this charming, antiques-filled ice cream parlor that I fell in love with coconut ice cream. Creamy and dense, intense yet not overbearing, the frozen delight was everything ice cream should be. From that first lick, my childhood favorite Baskin Robbin's boysenberry flavor was superseded. This homemade toasted coconut ice cream is super-simple to whip up, and may put your house on the map as a favorite ice cream destination for those who try it.

MAKES ABOUT 1 QUART

1 cup sweetened flaked coconut
1 1/4 cups canned cream of coconut, such as Coco Lopez
1/2 cup whole milk
1 1/2 cups heavy cream

1. Preheat the oven to 350°F. Spread the coconut evenly on a baking sheet and bake for 10 minutes, stirring after 5 minutes and thereafter as needed, until light golden brown.

2. Combine the cream of coconut, milk, and heavy cream in a saucepan and bring to a gentle boil. Simmer over medium-low heat, stirring constantly, for 10 minutes. Stir in the toasted coconut.

3. Chill for at least 4 hours in the refrigerator, then freeze in an ice cream maker according to the manufacturer's instructions.

PURE PEACH PIE

At some point every August, without fail, we come home to baskets of delicious, juicy peaches on our front porch, thanks to our most generous neighbors and their abundant peach trees. Because we are blessed with this fruitful bounty, we have enjoyed many peach pies over the years. MJ, our "peachy" neighbor, has guided my pie making, casually dropping helpful hints here and there: "I always keep one half of my dough chilled while rolling out the other portion;" or "I boil down my peach sauce for a better filling." Taking these tips into consideration (how could I not, MJ's pies are some of the best I've tasted), I've incorporated them into my standard peach pie recipe. The result: a heightened pure fruit flavor and a pie that's just peachy keen.

SERVES 8 TO 10

5 cups (about 2 pounds) peeled and
    thinly sliced peaches
$1/3$ cup plus 1 tablespoon sugar
2 tablespoons lemon juice
1 batch Flaky Pie Crust Dough (page 11)
$1/4$ cup brown sugar
2 tablespoons unsalted butter,
    cut into $1/4$-inch cubes
2 tablespoons all-purpose flour
2 tablespoons cornstarch
Pinch of salt

1. Toss the peaches, $1/3$ cup sugar, and lemon juice gently together in a bowl. Set aside to macerate for 45 minutes.

2. Meanwhile, let the dough sit for 10 minutes at room temperature before rolling out. (Take the dough out at staggered intervals, 5 minutes apart, which prevents the second disk from becoming too soft.) Preheat the oven to 425°F.

3. On a lightly floured surface, roll out the first disk to form a 12-inch circle and place on wax paper. Place the dough circle into a 9-inch pie plate. Roll out the second disk into an 11-inch circle. Chill the crusts while preparing the filling.

4. After the peaches have macerated, drain off the juices into a liquid measuring cup; you should yield at least ½ cup. Put all of the juices in a heavy saucepan and add the brown sugar. Boil over medium-high heat, without stirring, for 6 to 8 minutes or until the sauce is thickened and reduced by about one third. Remove from the heat and stir in the butter until completely melted.

5. Add the flour, cornstarch, and salt to the peaches and gently toss. Pour the reduced sauce on top and gently toss again.

6. Put the filling in the prepared crust and cover with the second dough circle. Seal the top dough edge to the bottom edge by wrapping the top under the bottom edge and crimping. Using a knife, make several vents in the top crust. Sprinkle with the remaining 1 tablespoon sugar.

7. Place the pie plate on an aluminum foil–covered baking sheet and bake for 50 to 55 minutes. After 20 minutes, or when the edges become brown, cover the pie with foil or a pie shield. Let cool for at least 2 hours before serving.

RHUBARB CRUMBLE BARS

A big, vegetable-rich garden is something I have always dreamed of. Many people in my extended family were farmers, so perhaps the desire is in my blood. My parents, however, did not share this passion. They made a half-hearted effort by tilling a tiny plot of land behind our white Colonial and planting a few tomato plants, Indian corn (a result of my badgering), gladiolas, and rhubarb. I still dream of a large garden. We now have a small one and grow mainly greens—lettuces, spinach, kale, chard, broccoli, and herbs—not the scores of squash, eggplant, and carrots that I'd like to plant, but as every major undertaking in life, it takes time. I understand now why my parents grew rhubarb; it's easy to care for and grows well. This recipe for thick, crumbly bars uses only rhubarb, no other fruit to tone down the tartness, which is balanced by a sweet dough. The large pan size makes enough to share—and is a good excuse to use up that extra rhubarb from a bountiful harvest.

MAKES 21 BARS
FILLING

6 cups rhubarb cut in 1/2-inch pieces
  (about 1 1/2 pounds)

1 cup firmly packed brown sugar

3 tablespoons cornstarch

2 teaspoons grated lemon zest

1 tablespoon orange juice

1/8 teaspoon salt

2 tablespoons cold unsalted butter, cut
  into 1/2-inch pieces

CRUST AND TOPPING

1 cup slivered almonds

1 cup old-fashioned rolled oats

2 cups all-purpose flour

1 teaspoon baking soda

1/4 teaspoon salt

1 cup sugar

8 ounces (2 sticks) cold
  unsalted butter, cut
  into 1-inch pieces

1 teaspoon pure vanilla extract

1. Preheat the oven to 350°F. Line a 9 x 13-inch pan with parchment paper, leaving a 1-inch overhang on each of the long sides. Spray the pan and parchment with baking spray.

2. Make the filling: Combine the rhubarb, brown sugar, cornstarch, lemon zest, orange juice, and salt together in a bowl. Stir well and set aside.

3. Make the crust: Put the almonds in the bowl of a food processor and run for about 20 seconds, or until the almonds are finely ground. Add the oats, flour, baking soda, salt, and sugar and pulse 12 times, or until combined. Add the butter and vanilla extract and run for about 2 minutes, or until the dough is thoroughly mixed and just starts to come together.

4. Put about half the dough, about 2 1/4 cups, in the prepared pan and gently press evenly over the entire bottom, using an offset spatula. Pour the rhubarb filling over the crust and dot with the 2 tablespoons butter.

5. Using your fingers, make some large clumps with the remaining dough and place them evenly over the rhubarb; sprinkle the rest of the dough crumbs over the filling so the entire surface is lightly covered with topping. Bake for 30 minutes, then increase the oven temperature to 375°F and bake for another 8 to 10 minutes, or until the crust is pale golden brown.

6. Let cool and cut into 2 x 3-inch rectangles. Use an offset spatula to remove the bars from the pan.

CRUNCHY LIME MINT COOKIES

This recipe, new to the fold, will I hope be a keeper in our family. While it has no history yet, the recipe has kept coming back to us over the past few years. My daughter, Anna, and I share a love of lime and mint and crave these cookies for the subtle presence of both flavors. People don't know what to expect when biting into this long, slender edible. To some, these cookies may resemble a savory cracker or biscuit due to the chopped mint in the glaze, which could easily be mistaken for cilantro. This is part of the cookie's charm, it's mysterious but one bite and the answer is clear: a deliciously sweet lime-mint cookie. I hope my kids will bake these with their children one day.

MAKES ABOUT 2½ TO 3 DOZEN COOKIES
LIME COOKIES

3 cups all-purpose flour

1½ teaspoons baking powder

1 teaspoon salt

8 ounces (2 sticks) unsalted butter,
   at room temperature

½ cup firmly packed light brown sugar

½ cup granulated sugar

2 large eggs plus 1 yolk, at room
   temperature

1 tablespoon grated lime zest (from
   about 1 small lime)

MINT LIME GLAZE

1 cup confectioners' sugar, sifted

3 tablespoons lime juice

2 teaspoons grated lime zest

2 tablespoons finely chopped fresh mint

Top: Dad's Chocolate Mudslide Cookies
Bottom: Cruncy Lime Mint Cookies

1. Make the lime cookies: Preheat the oven to 375°F. Line a baking sheet with parchment paper.

2. Stir together the flour, baking powder, and salt in a small bowl.

3. In the bowl of a food processor, combine the butter and sugars and process for 30 to 45 seconds, or until thoroughly combined. Add the whole eggs, the yolk, and the lime zest and pulse 8 to 10 times.

4. Add the flour mixture to the food processor and pulse 6 to 8 times or until the mixture comes together and forms a loose dough (it will not form a ball).

5. Turn the dough out onto a lightly floured surface and divide it into 3 parts. Using your hands, form each part into a 10 x 5-inch rectangle, about ³/8 inch thick. Using a knife, cut each rectangle into 8 diagonal strips (1-inch wide). There will be 8 because you'll lose a little on each end due to the diagonal cut. Cut each strip into 3-inch cookies. Place on the prepared baking sheet. Save the extra dough from each of the 3 sections and form a few more cookies. Chill the cookies on the baking sheet in the refrigerator for 15 minutes.

6. Bake the chilled cookies for 20 minutes or until the edges begin to turn the palest golden color. If you overbake the cookies, they lose their lime flavor and will taste just like a sugar cookie, but to get a crunch, they need to be baked thoroughly.

7. Remove from the oven and let cool for about 30 minutes on the baking sheet before moving to a wire rack set over wax paper.

8. Make the mint lime glaze: Stir together the confectioners' sugar, lime juice, and zest in a small bowl. Add the mint.

9. Generously spread the Mint Lime Glaze over the cookies, allowing any extra to drip down the sides of the cookies onto the wax paper.

DAD'S CHOCOLATE MUDSLIDE COOKIES

My father is an addict. His vices: crusty bread and dark chocolate—the darker the better. I know his compulsions could be worse, but his junkie-like behavior gets disruptive at times. One fine spring day our family was enjoying a lovely meal at the Culinary Institute of America in Hyde Park, New York. When the bread basket arrived, crackpot symptoms started. He couldn't get enough of the sourdough boule. I was downright embarrassed when after the sixth request, the waiter said there was no more and sent my father to the institution's bakery. Not only did he score three extra-crusty sourdough boules, he also had a gigantic chocolate mudslide cookie, which was extra-rich and chocolatey. He was guarding his stash with such intensity I knew one cookie would not suffice. We would have to re-create this chocolate addict's dream. This cookie, adapted from the CIA's Mudslide Cookie, is deceptively light in texture for its rich chocolate flavor. The higher quality chocolate you use, the more intense the flavor. I favor Scharffen Berger, which also makes cacao nibs, which I've added to this cookie.

MAKES 30 COOKIES

3/4 cup plus 2 tablespoons cake flour

1 tablespoon baking powder

1/4 teaspoon salt

6 ounces unsweetened chocolate, coarsely chopped

7 ounces bittersweet chocolate, coarsely chopped

8 tablespoons (1 stick) unsalted butter

2 teaspoons instant espresso powder

1 tablespoon boiling water

7 large eggs, at room temperature

2 3/4 cups sugar

1 teaspoon pure vanilla extract

1 1/2 cups bittersweet chocolate chips, such as Ghiradelli 60% cacao

1/2 cup cacao nibs

1 1/2 cups pecans, chopped (optional)

1. Preheat the oven to 350°F. Line two baking sheets with parchment paper.

2. In a small bowl, sift together the flour, baking powder, and salt. Set aside.

3. In a small saucepan over low heat, melt the unsweetened and bittersweet chocolates and butter, stirring constantly until completely blended together. Remove from the heat and let cool.

4. In another small bowl, stir together the espresso powder and boiling water.

5. In the bowl of a stand mixer fitted with the whisk attachment, beat the eggs and sugar together on medium-high until thick,

Cacao nibs, crushed pieces of ROASTED COCOA BEANS, add a SURPRISING CRUNCH and are a good nut replacement (although if you add the optional nuts to this cookie it just makes them DOUBLY GOOD). Nibs can be hard to find, and somewhat pricey, but WORTH THE TIME and money. There are many online suppliers, including MY FAVORITE Scharffen Berger's worldpantry.com. You could also check Whole Foods or your local health food store.

voluminous, and light yellow, about 3 minutes. Stir in the espresso and vanilla extract. Add the melted butter-chocolate mixture. Beat until combined, less than 1 minute.

6. With the mixer on low, add the dry ingredients and beat until just combined. Fold in the chocolate chips and cacao nibs, and nuts if desired.

7. Fill a $1/4$-cup measure with batter and place scoops 3 inches apart on the prepared baking sheets. Bake for 15 minutes. Let cool for 10 minutes on the baking sheets before moving the cookies to a cooling rack using a spatula.

FFRENCH FROMAGE BLANC

Probably the simplest dessert in this book, Ffrench Fromage Blanc was inspired by my husband, who adores this white French cheese for dessert. A no-fuss kind of guy, he likes it nearly unadorned, with just a drizzle of honey to complement the cheese's tangy edge. Fromage blanc, a crème fraîche–, yogurt-like dairy product, may be made at home, but is available ready-made in most supermarkets. This creamy cheese is the perfect complement to any fruit, and will take you mere seconds to dish out onto dessert plates. And doesn't it sound fancier to serve fruit with fromage blanc than just plain old yogurt?

SERVES 8
Two 8-ounce containers fromage blanc
1 cup cherries, pitted and halved
1 fresh apricot, cut into $1/2$-inch pieces
$1/2$ cup cherry preserves
$1/2$ cup honey

1. Divide the fromage blanc, cherries, and apricot among 8 plates ($1/4$ cup each of cheese and fruit per plate).

2. Heat the preserves over low heat until warm and thinned.

3. Spoon 1 tablespoon preserves and honey over each plate of cheese and fruit and serve.

LOVE STRUCK SOUR CHERRY PIE

⧖

"Sour cherries? What's the big deal about sour cherries?" I asked my neighbor Robin, who had just returned from a two-hour round-trip excursion along the Hudson River to purchase this fruit, which was quite unfamiliar to me. She just looked my way, rolled her eyes, and said, "I'll be by later with something good—really good." A sour cherry virgin, I was taken by complete surprise when my friend returned with a slice of pie, red, gleaming fruit peeking out from under a golden, flaky crust. With the first taste I was struck, as if by an arrow from Cupid's bow. This was no childlike crush—I was bewitched, enraptured, love struck. Now when late June approaches, like the sugary filling of a pie, my eyes become glazed at the thought of sour cherries, which, in the Hudson Valley, come into season for just a few fleeting weeks in July. I, too, will now drive crazy distances seeking out this small, bright red, almost translucent stone fruit. This recipe, for sour cherry pie with a crust of hearts, brings out the flavor of my favorite fruit beautifully. I hope you, too, will feel the love.

SERVES 8 TO 10

6 cups sour cherries, pitted

1 1/4 cups sugar

2 tablespoons cornstarch

2 tablespoons quick-cooking tapioca

1 teaspoon lemon juice

1 batch Flaky Pie Crust Dough (page 11)

2 tablespoons unsalted butter, cut into 1/2-inch pieces

1. Combine the cherries, sugar, cornstarch, tapioca, and lemon juice in a bowl and toss gently. Set aside.

2. Turn the dough out onto lightly floured parchment paper and divide into 2 equal portions. Using a lightly floured rolling pin, roll out one dough portion 1/8 inch thick and wide enough to cut a 12-inch circle. Fold the dough circle in half and carefully place in a 9-inch pie plate. Unfold. Crimp or pinch the edges of the crust.

3. Roll out the remaining dough to 1/8 inch thick. Cut the dough using heart-shape cookie cutters. Set aside.

4. Pour the filling into the prepared crust. Dot the filling with small pieces of butter. Cover most of the filling with the dough hearts arranged in a decorative pattern from the edges to the center. Chill the entire pie for 1 hour in the refrigerator.

5. Preheat the oven to 400°F.

6. Place the pie plate on an aluminum foil–lined baking sheet on the middle oven rack. After 15 minutes, place a pie crust shield on the pie to protect the edges from becoming too brown. After another 15 minutes (30 minutes of baking time), check to see if the pie crust is becoming golden. If necessary, cover loosely with aluminum foil to prevent burning. Continue to bake until the filling is thick and bubbly, 40 to 45 minutes total.

7. Let cool for at least 2 hours before serving.

MIXED BERRY KICKSAWS

After a field trip to the Hudson Valley's Van Cortlandt Manor, an eighteenth-century farm and historic property, Camilla was brimming with excitement. She wanted to teach me what she'd learned that day from a costumed guide: how to make kickshaws. "There's no recipe, Mommy," she told me, "let me show you how…it's easy." She proceeded to relay the day's events while using her hands to mix butter with flour. "Make sure the butter is the size of peas," she said, "…and don't flatten the lumps, Mommy, make sure they stay round." She was making pie dough with her hands, Colonial-style. I loved that fact that she didn't feel wedded to a recipe's proportions. She said you just have to "feel the dough ´til it's right." Once the dough is done, you roll it out and use a glass to cut circles, fill them with a "smidge" of jam, to quote Camilla, fold them in half, then bake or fry the half moons. The result is a small, sweet hand pie. I look to my children often for inspiration, admiring their sense of freedom and confidence.

MAKES 20 3-INCH PIES

1 1/4 cups all-purpose flour

1/2 teaspoon salt

8 tablespoons (1 stick) cold unsalted
   butter, cut into 1/4-inch cubes

3 tablespoons ice-cold water

1/4 cup Sweet Blackberry Jam (see
   opposite, or choose your favorite
   fruit flavor)

Sugar for sprinkling

1. Preheat the oven to 375°F. Line a baking sheet with parchment paper.

2. Mix the flour and salt together in a bowl. Blend in the butter using your fingers until the butter is the size of peas. Slowly add the ice-cold water while continuing to mix the dough with your hands. The dough should not be sticky.

3. Using a rolling pin, roll the dough out on a floured surface about 1/4 inch thick. With a drinking glass, cut the dough into circles.

4. Place a very small spoonful of jam in the center of each dough circle, fold in half, and pinch the edges together. Place the kickshaws on the prepared baking sheet and sprinkle with sugar.

5. Bake for 30 minutes, or until golden brown. Let cool slightly before serving.

SWEET BLACKBERRY JAM

I felt like the luckiest kid in the world. My childhood home had woods to play in, a pond to boat in, and a huge patch of wild black raspberries to eat. As I greedily reached for the sweet, juicy berries, I'd forget about the prickers and would inevitably have red, scratched arms for a week or two in summer. On the other hand, my sensible mother would cover herself from head to toe before approaching the thorny bramble. Armed as she was, she would return to the house with a basketful of the berries (I never made it that far). If she gathered enough, she'd make a pie or jam. Freezer jam is her preferred method. I like to cook my jam instead because it requires less sugar—and I use blackberries because unfortunately my parents moved from that house long ago, and black raspberries are scarcely available in markets. Red raspberries are a great option for this recipe as well.

MAKES 6 HALF-PINT JARS

8 cups (about 1 quart) fresh blackberries
1 tablespoon freshly squeezed
    lemon juice
3 cups sugar

PECTIN is a GELLING AGENT that occurs naturally in fruits such as APPLES and LEMONS. Commercially prepared fruit pectin, such as Sure Jell and Ball, are available in dry or liquid forms. Most packages offer recipes, but many require LOADS OF SUGAR. If you like a thicker jam, add 4 tablespoons pectin to this recipe right after you MASH THE BERRIES and cook as directed. Perhaps try a batch both ways and see WHICH YOU PREFER.

1. Place a small plate in the freezer. Sterilize 6 half-pint jars in the dishwasher or hand wash them. Place a rack or towel in the bottom of a Dutch oven and put the jars and lids on top and cover with water. Bring to a boil, remove from the heat, and set aside.

2. Rinse the berries and put them in a 6- to 8-quart saucepan. Mash lightly with a potato masher and add the lemon juice. Bring to a boil over medium heat. Add the sugar, stir until completely dissolved, and boil over medium heat for 15 to 20 minutes, stirring occasionally, and skimming off the foam as needed.

3. To test the jam's gel point, remove the plate from the freezer, place a spoonful of hot jam on it, and return it to the freezer for a minute. Run your finger through the jam to see if it gels or resists. If not, continue to boil for a few more minutes and retest the jam.

4. Remove the jars from the water and turn upright on the counter. When the jam has reached its gel point, ladle it into the jars, leaving about ¼ inch from the top of each jar. Wipe the jars clean and cover tightly using sealed lids. Put the jars back in the Dutch oven, making sure the water covers the jars by at least one inch. Bring the water to a boil, and at that point, continue to boil for 15 more minutes. Remove the jars from the water and let cool. The lid should not pop back when pressed. If it does, the jar is not properly sealed and should be refrigerated. Store properly sealed jars for up to one year in a cool, dry place.

ALMOND BLACKBERRY TORTE

A very good family friend, John MacAlpine, started baking late in life. He was way into his sixties when he started producing more cakes, pies, and tarts than his family could eat. Maybe he was making up for lost time, because there was no keeping John out of the kitchen. Having dessert at the MacAlpine's house after a holiday meal is akin to eating another whole meal. The entire dining room table is reset with desserts, fruits, and sauces, accompanied by small handwritten tags describing each dish—a true dessert buffet. This blackberry torte was inspired by the many types that have bedecked the MacAlpine table over the years: raspberry, almond, and mocha walnut to name a few. For those who feel it's too late to start baking, look to John, who, without sounding trite, has proven it's never too late.

SERVES 8 TO 10

CRUST

1 1/3 cups all-purpose flour

1 teaspoon baking powder

1/3 cup sugar

1/2 teaspoon pure almond extract

8 tablespoons (1 stick) unsalted butter

1 large egg, lightly beaten

1/2 cup blackberry preserves

FILLING

3 large eggs, separated

1 cup slivered almonds

8 tablespoons (1 stick) unsalted butter,
    at room temperature

1/3 cup sugar

1/8 teaspoon pure almond extract

SAUCE

1 cup fresh blackberries plus extra
    for garnish

1/3 cup sugar

1 tablespoon lemon juice

2 teaspoons crème de cassis

1. Grease a 10-inch springform pan with baking spray.

2. Make the crust: In the bowl of a food processor, combine the flour, baking powder, and sugar. Pulse several times. Add the almond extract and butter. Run for about 15 seconds, or until the butter is fully incorporated. Add the egg and run again until the dough just comes together, 10 to 15 seconds.

3. Using your fingers, press the dough into the bottom of the prepared pan. If the dough is sticky, flour your fingers.

4. Spread the dough with the blackberry preserves. Place the pan in the refrigerator to chill.

5. Preheat the oven to 425°F.

6. Meanwhile, make the filling: Beat the egg whites until soft peaks form. Set aside.

7. Put the almonds in the bowl of a food processor and pulse 6 to 8 times, or until ground. Add the butter, sugar, egg yolks, and almond extract. Process until thoroughly combined. Transfer to a mixing bowl and fold in half the egg whites until incorporated. Continue to fold in the rest of the egg whites.

8. Remove the crust from the fridge and spread the egg mixture on top. Bake for 20 minutes. Cover with foil and bake for another 10 to 15 minutes. Let cool.

9. Make the sauce: Put the blackberries, sugar, lemon juice, and crème de cassis in the bowl of a food processor and run until the mixture is smooth.

10. Push the sauce through a fine sieve and discard any seeds. Serve the sauce over thin wedges of the torte.

INDEX

ACKNOWLEDGMENTS

My heartfelt thanks goes to all those who have shared their recipes and taught me along the way. I'd like to thank my good friend Chelsea Mauldin for encouraging me, Kathleen Hackett for pointing me in the right direction, and Sharon Bowers, my phenomenal agent who has taken me under her wing and given me endless support. I'd like to also thank Anja Schmidt, editor extraordinaire—you're a dream to work. I am extremely appreciative to the rest of the exceptional team at Kyle Books and to Ron Longe. Thanks to the ideal photo-food styling team of the talented Philip Ficks, ingenious Rosco Betsill, Naomi McColloch, Robert Hessler, Peter Occolowitz and Maya Steward. A huge thanks to Chanda Chapin and Robin Chess for props, and to Rhonda and Camilla at Rhinebeck's Hammertown for their gorgeous housewares. Thanks also go to Jen Holz, Daikin Morehouse, Tom Comerford, Maureen and Serine at Papertrail and Williams-Sonoma for their generosity.

I am ever grateful for my infinitely kind neighbors: Julia Rose and Maya, the Rosenthals, and the Reisses for opening up their home and hearts to us. I am also appreciative to Robin and Marshall Chess who have done the same, and become family. A huge thanks to friends-cum-family Kylie (my devoted tester and kid minder), Michael, Sophia and Eric Brauer. I'd also like to thank Rebecca Shim and her staff for their care and good food. Great thanks to my cheerleaders Peter Jung and Andy Valdaliso.

All books are collaborations, but this one would not exist without my family—past and present—especially my grandmother Aline. My undying gratitude goes to both my mother and father for their unconditional love and support. They taught me to appreciate food while they fed my creativity. I'd also like to thank the Lanier family for their support and contributions, and especially Lisa, for rallying testers. My thanks to Aunt Sue and Aunt Bonnie for recipes and photos, to David (Da) Ffrench for reliving Jamaica with us, Renee, whose spirit is alive and well in this book, and Betsy Ffrench for her contributions. I'd like to extensively thank the many others who shared their recipes: Oliver Bailey, Jenny Bella, Hannah Borgeson, Judith Bromley, Lynn Fliegel, Jeanne Kiel, Heidi LaMonda, Jeanne and John MacAlpine, Ann McGillicuddy, Melissa and John Thongs, La Scanlon. Tusen takk to those Norwegians for their inspiration: the Neumann-Trellavik family and to Charlotte Haukedal, who taught me to make boller.

I've already named many from my terrific team of testers above, but there are still more to thank for their meticulous work including Stacy Bereck Chernosky, Christine Downs, Edgar Freer, Becky Grandone, Elizabeth and Ethan Gundeck, Eugenia Krause, Dana Kellman, Joanne Konrath, Morgan Lanier, Dale Mindack, Carolyn Nopar, Maxanne Resnick, Lisa, Ben and Josh Rosenkranz, Laura Walker, Ingrid White and Ann Williams. Many thanks go to my tasters at Poughkeepsie Day School, particularly Brian Reid's and Shirley Rinalidi's classes.

And I thank Anna and Camilla for their warmth, grace, and humor—and for embracing this adventure, happily living through shoots and becoming part of the project. And to my dearest Jim, who has taught me much. I thank him for being the kindest friend, most patient supporter, and truly the greatest partner.